13

D0933101

The World
from
1450 to 1700

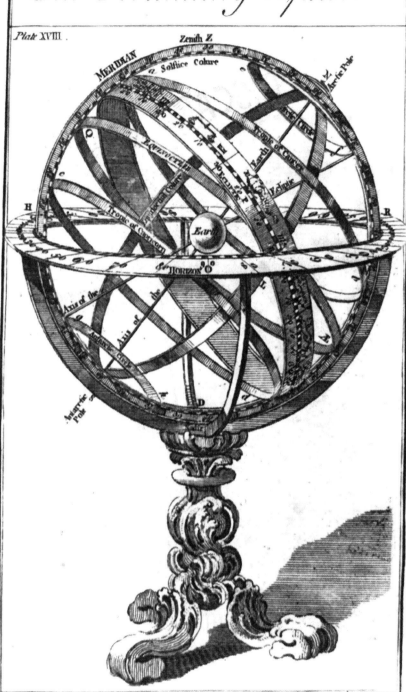

The
New
Oxford
World
History

The World
from
1450 to 1700

John E. Wills Jr.

OXFORD
UNIVERSITY PRESS

2009

OXFORD

UNIVERSITY PRESS

Oxford University Press, Inc., publishes works that further
Oxford University's objective of excellence
in research, scholarship, and education.

Oxford   New York
Auckland   Cape Town   Dar es Salaam   Hong Kong   Karachi
Kuala Lumpur   Madrid   Melbourne   Mexico City   Nairobi
New Delhi   Shanghai   Taipei   Toronto

With offices in
Argentina   Austria   Brazil   Chile   Czech Republic   France   Greece
Guatemala   Hungary   Italy   Japan   Poland   Portugal   Singapore
South Korea   Switzerland   Thailand   Turkey   Ukraine   Vietnam

Published by Oxford University Press, Inc.
198 Madison Avenue, New York, NY 10016

www.oup.com

Oxford is a registered trademark of Oxford University Press.

Library of Congress Cataloging-in-Publication Data
Wills, John E. (John Elliot), 1936–
The world from 1450 to 1700 / John E. Wills, Jr.
p.   cm.
Includes index.
Summary: "Traces the interwoven changes that led from the world of
Columbus, Luther, and the Mughal emperor Babur to the world of
Locke, Louis XIV, and the Kangxi Emperor. Wills encourages his readers
to acknowledge the special features of the European experience and
achievement without presenting Europe as essentially the only source of
the modern."—Provided by publisher.
ISBN 978-0-19-533797-6 (pbk.)—ISBN 978-0-19-516517-3 (hardcover)
1. History, Modern.   2. Europe–History.   I. Title.
D228.W53 2009
909.08—dc22
2009005806

Printed in the United States of America
on acid-free paper

Frontispiece: Armillary of the world, 18th century.
Library of Congress, LC-USZ62-87905.

*To my colleagues at the University
of Southern California*

Contents

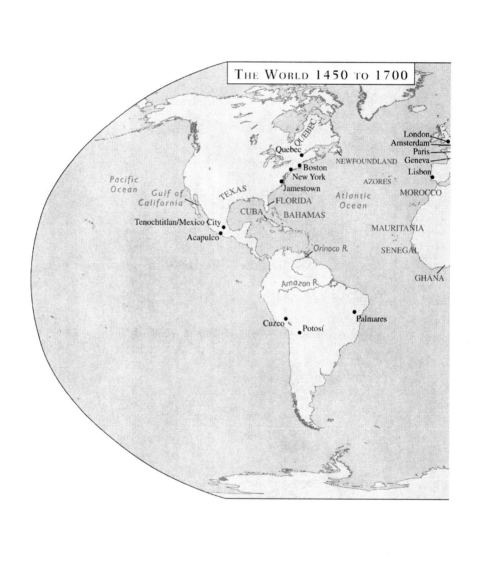

THE WORLD 1450 TO 1700

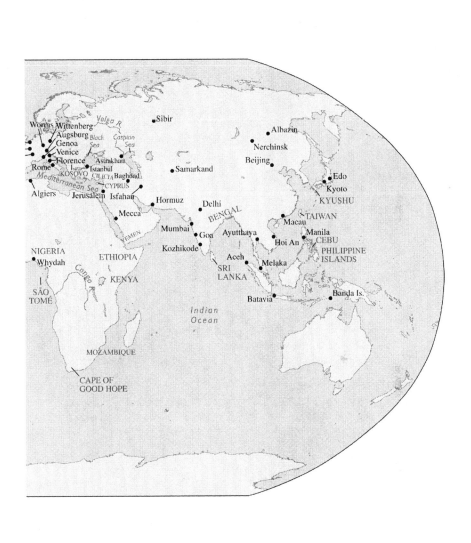

Editors' Preface

This book is part of the New Oxford World History, an innovative series that offers readers an informed, lively, and up-to-date history of the world and its people that represents a significant change from the "old" world history. Only a few years ago, world history generally amounted to a history of the West—Europe and the United States—with small amounts of information about the rest of the world. Some versions of the old world history drew attention to every part of the world *except* Europe and the United States. Readers of that kind of world history might get the impression that somehow the rest of the world was made up of exotic people who had strange customs and spoke difficult languages. Still another kind of "old" world history presented the story of areas or peoples of the world by focusing primarily on the achievements of great civilizations. Readers learned of great buildings, influential world religions, and mighty rulers but little of ordinary people or more general economic and social patterns. Interactions among the world's peoples were often told from only one perspective.

This series has a different perspective on world history. First, it is comprehensive, covering all countries and regions of the world and investigating the total human experience—even those of so-called "peoples without histories" living far from the great civilizations. "New" world historians thus share an interest in all of human history, even going back millions of years before there were written human records. A few "new" world histories even extend their focus to the entire universe, a "big history" perspective that dramatically shifts the beginning of the story back to the Big Bang. Some see the "new" global framework of world history today in terms of viewing the world from the vantage point of the moon, as one scholar put it. We agree. But we also want to take a close-up view, analyzing and reconstructing the significant experiences of all of humanity.

This is not to say that everything that has happened everywhere and in all time periods can be recovered or is worth knowing, but that there is much to be gained by considering both the separate and interrelated stories of different societies and cultures. Making these connections is still another crucial ingredient of the "new" world history. It emphasizes connectedness and interactions of all kinds—cultural, economic, political, religious, and social—involving peoples, places, and processes. It makes comparisons and finds similarities. Emphasizing both the comparisons and interactions is critical to developing a global framework that can deepen and broaden historical understanding, whether the focus is on a specific country or region or on the whole world.

The rise of the new world history as a discipline comes at an opportune time. The interest in world history in schools and among the general public is vast. We travel to one another's nations, converse and work with people around the world, and are changed by global events. War and peace affect populations worldwide as do economic conditions and the state of our environment, communications, and health and medicine. The New Oxford World History presents local histories in a global context and provides an overview of world events seen through the eyes of ordinary people. This combination of the local and the global further defines the new world history. Understanding the workings of global and local conditions in the past enables us to examine our own world and to envision the interconnected future that is in the making.

Bonnie G. Smith
Anand Yang

The World
from
1450 to 1700

Prologue: Texas and the World

On June 17, 1527, a squadron of five ships with about six hundred men aboard set out from the port of San Lucar de Barrameda in southern Spain. The commander, Pámphilo de Narváez, had a royal commission to "conquer and govern" lands along the north side of the Gulf of Mexico from the peninsula that now is Florida to about the Texas-Mexico border. Other Spaniards were named to lesser offices in the planned colony, and there were several Franciscan priests on board. There is no evidence that the Native American inhabitants of these lands would have any say as to who ruled them. The pope had divided the world between the Spanish and the Portuguese monarchies. Most Roman Catholics believed that the pope was God's deputy on earth, the head of the one true church. Charles V, King of Spain and Holy Roman Emperor, was just beginning his long years of bitter struggle against the challenges to Catholicism of Martin Luther and his followers. Anyone on the voyage over thirty-five had been born in a Spain still at war with a Muslim monarchy in its midst, at Granada, and the tensions between Spanish Catholics and Spaniards of Muslim and of Jewish heritage gave an unusually militant character to Spanish Catholicism. Piracy and slave-raiding across the Mediterranean, between its Catholic northern and Muslim southern shores, also shaped people's attitudes. Some of the leaders of the expedition brought an African slave or two along to serve them.

The expedition sailed into a Caribbean already transformed by more than thirty years of Spanish occupation and exploitation, by European diseases to which Native Americans had no resistance, and by the improbable triumph of Hernán Cortés and his forces over the great Aztec Empire, a triumph that no doubt was the model for what Narváez and his followers hoped to accomplish. They sailed straight into the Caribbean hurricane season, even more dangerous for wooden sailing ships than it is in modern times, and were lucky to survive several storms as they took on more horses and supplies in Cuba. In April 1528, when they finally landed on the shores of the planned colony, somewhere near Tampa Bay, the thin veneer of royal appointment and orderly procedure shattered, and they started yelling at each other. They had no idea where they were. They found only a few small Native American settlements, no gold, and no crops to extort or steal. Narváez wanted to lead his forces to explore inland, the ships coasting along until they found a good harbor where they could meet again. He prevailed against the better judgment of others. The ships sailed away, and the party on the ships spent most of the next year searching up and down the coast for the land party, never finding it. About three hundred men under Narváez made their way across swamps and coastal bays, occasionally finding corn to steal in a Native American village. By July 1528 they were in the area of modern Apalachee Bay, near Tallahassee, and were under constant attack from native warriors. In August and September, in an amazing display of improvised use of materials—shirts sewn into sails, stirrups made into nails—they built five small, low-sided sailing ships and set off west along down the gulf coast. They almost starved. A few, driven mad by thirst, drank salt water and died. Of the two hundred and fifty or so who set out, about eighty were still alive when they reached the Texas coast, somewhere near modern Galveston, around November 1. By February 1529 only fifteen were alive. In one group of five stranded on an island, the survivors had eaten the dead until only one remained.

The local Native American peoples, Karankawa and related groups, were appalled to find cannibals on their shores but struck by pity at the sight of Spaniards starving, cold, almost naked. They took them into their settlements, shared their meager food with them, and insisted that the Spaniards share the work of gathering firewood, digging roots, and so on. This was the beginning of eight years of a rare kind of encounter, between European observers who were completely at the mercy of their Native American hosts and a people whose hunter-gatherer way of life had scarcely been affected by European contact. We know about it because one of the Spaniards who survived to return to the Spanish-speaking world was the literate and remarkably observant treasurer of the projected colony, Álvar Núñez Cabeza de Vaca. His account of his adventures is as good a place as any to start thinking about the world of the 1500s, since it links world-transforming innovations with man's oldest way of life, that of the hunter-gatherer.

The Native American peoples of southern Texas planted nothing and had no domestic animals. They depended completely on a cycle of food available at different places at different times of the year. Late in the spring they spent several months feasting on oysters by the coastal lagoons, camped on great piles of oyster shells left from centuries of such feasting. They also found ripe berries in the coastal thickets. A bit later they had a few weeks of good eating from the pecan groves along the coastal rivers. Then they headed inland to the forbidding thorny mesquite plains, where the fruit of the prickly pear cactus ripened in late summer, the best part of their year. But in winter food was in very short supply, and cold winds whipped down the huge continent from the north. Cabeza de Vaca, as unclothed as they were, sharing their feasts and their famines, was very much impressed with their knowledge of the seasons and of the resources of their environment.

Soon after their arrival on the Texas coast, the Spaniards discovered that the Native Americans expected the strangers could cure illnesses. "The same night we arrived there came some Indians to Castillo and they told him they were sick in the head, begging him to cure them, and after he had made the sign of the cross over them and commended them to God, in that moment the Indians said that all the illness had left them, [and they brought them gifts of deer meat and other food.]…. And after the cures were finished they began to dance and to make their songs and celebrations until the sun came up the next day, and the celebration lasted three days, in honor of our coming."[1] The Spaniards did what they could, saying little prayers and making the sign of the cross, and sometimes people got better. These people lived in small groups of related families, with few distinctions of power or prestige. The only people who had a special place in the community were the healers. Drawing on hints in Cabeza de Vaca's account and other sources, it seems likely that the dependence on seasonal food resources produced episodes of binge eating of very different and sometimes not very healthy kinds of food. The result seems to have been frequent bloating and intestinal distress, from which most people recovered within a few days. An elder, someone who had special dreams, or a woman with healing hands would say a spell at the right time and become a trusted healer. And the Spaniards, with their big noses, pale skins, and beards, obviously were from some other realm, and of course they too were asked to heal. The Karankawa had taken the Spaniards in out of charity, but they were not going to let them walk away if they were healers or could be traded for valuable goods.

The Native American peoples frequently fought with each other, but they also had wide trade networks. Nuts and shells from the coast might be traded for a buffalo hide from the plains to the north. Women could continue to trade even when their men were trying to kill each other. So could weird strangers; Cabeza de Vaca improved his own life and broadened his knowledge of the local people by becoming a trader. Finally, by 1533 or 1534 there were only three Spaniards and one African slave left from the original expedition. At the grounds of the big prickly pear feast they managed to get away from the Karankawa and join another group. They hoped to go to the south and west and eventually make it to a Spanish settlement. The slave, always simply called Estebánico, or Little Steven, seems to have been unusually adept at figuring out where they were and at building good relations with the Native American peoples.

But at the core of those relations was the expectation of healing. News of the Spaniards' healing powers spread along trade networks, especially when different groups met at the best stands of prickly pear. When a Native American group guided the Spaniards to a new village, the people swarmed to meet them, touch them, and be healed. The Native American people who had brought them insisted on big presents from the new hosts, or simply stole from them. Then, after a spell of touching, healing, and wild celebration, the new hosts recouped their losses by taking the strangers to yet another group and getting goods from them in return.

Swept along by this extraordinary process, the three Spaniards and one African slave decided to turn away from the Gulf of Mexico and to make their way all the way across what is now northern Mexico to the Gulf of California. They encountered some larger villages where maize, beans, and squash were grown. Coming out near Spanish settlements on the coastal plain of the Gulf of California about the end of 1535, they were appalled to find frontier Spaniards raiding Native American communities to take slaves. They managed to work out a truce that allowed the natives to live at peace in their villages for some time and allowed Cabeza de Vaca and his three companions to make their way in July 1536, eight years after their arrival on the Texas coast, to Mexico City, where they were greeted by the Spanish viceroy and the great conqueror Cortés.

The huge and varied land we now call Texas would seem to be far off on the margins of the big changes we will be tracing in this book. That is a good reason to start there. We need to remember that some people facing these changes with limited resources or having the bad luck to be in the way of a big change simply disappeared. No one today claims to be descended from the Karankawa. Other Native American peoples managed to preserve their ways of life in the face of great losses of life to alien diseases and the challenges and opportunities of new connections with the wider world.

For example, in the woodlands of what is now eastern Texas the Caddo had an ordered way of life with regular cooperation in farming and house-building, grave deliberation in governing, good order, and lack of crime in their towns, a situation that few parts of Europe could have matched in 1500 or 1600. It is clear that they had lost many people to disease by 1600, but somehow they had maintained the integrity of their way of life. Growing corn, beans, pumpkins, squash, berries, and fruit in the good soil and mild climate, fishing and hunting deer and bear, they were less likely to go to bed hungry than peasants in many parts of Europe. Acknowledging a god in heaven, lighting all their fires from a perpetual sacred fire in a special temple, sending off their dead with moving ceremony, they followed a cycle of rites tied to the agricultural year. They made beautiful baskets and reed mats, sturdy leather clothing, and some of the finest pottery of aboriginal North America. By the late 1600s they were getting trade goods from French settlements to the east, and horses—descendants of those brought by the Spanish—from the Spanish or from the tribes of the plains to the west. They were quite confident of their ability to welcome French or Spanish visitors, playing one off against the other, without losing control of the situation. Later they won the respect even of the early missionaries who wanted to change their way of life at its roots. It was only as they were surrounded and swamped by the tide of Euro-American settlement after 1750 that they began a sharp decline; today they survive only on a tiny reservation in Oklahoma.

By 1680 the Caddo had obtained horses, but this did not change their lifestyle. Out on the great treeless plains that stretched to the Rocky Mountains across what is now west Texas and the Panhandle, native peoples by 1700 were creating a new way of life centered on horsemanship, warfare, and hunting buffalo. They were the southernmost-and among the first-to create the "Plains Indian" way of life that persisted until the late 1800s and has a hold on the modern imagination, especially by way of Hollywood Westerns, to this day.

Until well after 1600 these southern peoples farmed part of the year and hunted buffalo after the harvest. Hunting the big, swift buffalo on foot was at best a risky business. It seems likely that some Native American people began to buy or steal horses from the new Spanish settlements along the upper Rio Grande, near modern Santa Fe, New Mexico, in the early 1600s. When the Pueblo people of that area drove the Spaniards out temporarily in 1680, they did not have much use for their herds of horses since they were farmers; they probably traded the animals to the people out on the plains. By 1700 the Native Americans of the plains were raiding the Rio Grande valley settlements. Among them were Apaches and soon Comanches, the most feared Native American warriors until the late 1800s. These Texas plains were at the southern end of the range of the great herds of buffalo, but there were enough to allow these people to maintain a full and exciting nomadic way of life, moving all their goods from camp to camp on poles dragged by the horses, getting all they needed—meat, skins for tents and clothes, and much more—from the buffalo pursued and shot or lanced from horse-back, winning fame as warriors in fights with neighboring peoples.

This book spans the globe, looks at some big changes, asks some big questions about how our world got into its present interconnected and troubled state, and tells the stories of some amazing people, famous and infamous. But it's a good idea to begin with small stories based on a few shreds of evidence, about people and places far from the big, dramatic transformations. Much of what we think we know about the past is built on one or two texts, many of them even harder to figure out than Cabeza de Vaca's. History is made by the changes and choices of the most ordinary, even obscure, people, not just great men and women.

CHAPTER I

Islam and a Wider World, 1450–1490

Haya ʻalas Salat…Haya ʻalal-Falah. Allahu Akbar. La ilaha illa Allah…Come to prayer…Come to prayer…God is Great…There is no God but God. For weeks in the spring of 1453 the Christian soldiers, Greeks, and their allies who were manning the great double walls of Constantinople had heard at dawn the Muslim call to prayer from the siege lines of the Ottoman Turkish armies that faced them. The Ottoman forces outnumbered the defenders at least four to one, perhaps ten to one, and were far better organized. They had brought in materials by ship and built in a few weeks a strong stone fortress at the narrowest point of the Bosporus, the key strait between Constantinople and the Black Sea. They had built a wooden slipway and moved small ships overland into an inner harbor, bypassing a great chain protecting it. Their cannon were bigger and more intelligently used than anything inside the city. Several times the cannon had shattered a piece of the great walls, but each time the defenders had managed to repair the breach, which must have given the defenders some hope that God was on their side after all. In the city, religious services and processions, with the glorious singing of the Greek Orthodox tradition and the glowing colors of the icons, the sacred images of Jesus, the Virgin Mary, and the saints, never stopped.

But on May 12 the holiest icon slipped from its platform during a procession, and the next day was full of fog and strange light around the great Cathedral of the Holy Wisdom. The Ottomans said it was the true light of Islam that soon would shine there and eventually decided on a final massive attack. An Italian eyewitness, Giacomo Tedaldi, wrote: "After the Sultan had decided to make this further assault, he gave orders three days before the attack that there should be a solemn fast through the whole of his camp to honor and show reverence for the great God of Heaven, whom they worship alone. So he and his men fasted for three consecutive days, eating nothing throughout the day, but only at night time, under penalty of death. And by night they made lights with candles and wood, which were left to burn on land and on the water, so that it seemed that sea and land were on fire, with a great deal of noise from drums and other instruments (they have hardly any trumpets)."[1]

The final assault came in the dawn hours of May 29. It was a victory of Ottoman military discipline more than big guns, which in those hours made only small breaches in the walls around two of the great gates. After several advances were thrown back, Sultan Mehmet himself advanced with three thousand of his palace troops. He stood aside as they advanced silently, in perfect ranks. One side gate had not been properly secured, and about fifty attackers were able to get through it and up on the wall to plant their flag. They were cut off and in danger of annihilation when an Italian commander leading his men to help defend the city was shot, withdrew to the rear, and his men and the other defenders, deprived of their brave leader, began to panic. Ottoman forces now forced their way through two gates, and the defenses collapsed. Ottoman soldiers spread out to stop the general looting.

The young Sultan Mehmet rode through the breach in the massive double walls. His party moved through the streets of the great city directly to the splendid Church of the Holy Wisdom. He was not moved by the deep colors and glittering gold of the mosaics in the multiple domes; in Islamic belief man was said to blaspheme against the supreme power of the creator when he tried to make images of life and natural beauty, and even more when he set up a human presence, like Jesus or the Virgin Mary, to be worshipped in association with the one true god. The sultan brusquely gave orders to stop the soldiers who were getting out of hand and starting to tear up the magnificent marble pavement, and rode on to confer with the patriarch of the Greek Orthodox Church.

Thus, although Islam often seeks its own purity and resists influences from the non-Muslim world, here at this moment of triumph its leader already was dealing effectively with a complicated non-Muslim world, as were many Muslims, rulers, soldiers, merchants, and scholars, from the beginning of Islam to our own times. In their discipline, their use of big guns, their effective governmental organization, tolerance of non-Muslims under their rule, even in the way Islam considers all believers equal before the one God, they were not modern, but perhaps "early modern."

The conquest of Constantinople, soon to be known as Istanbul, by the Ottoman Turks had been a long time coming. The Ottomans had come out of the eastern edge of what is now Turkey before 1100, crossed into Europe in the 1340s, and by 1389 had won a great victory over the

Troops of Mehmet the Conqueror attack a Venetian fortress on the Bosporus around 1450. The Ottoman artist highlights the abundant firearms and good organization of the attackers. Bildarchiv Preussischer Kulturbesitz / Art Resource, NY.

Serbs at Kosovo, which remains in Serb nationalist memory to this day as the day when the Serbs were the brave front line of Christian Europe against the Muslim hordes. Still, the great powers of Europe had failed to overcome the old split between Roman Catholicism, which gave the pope in Rome authority over all Christians, and Greek Orthodoxy, centered in Constantinople, which rejected that claim. They had failed to organize anything like an adequate counter-attack, and in general had remained in denial about the scope of the Ottoman threat.

Constantinople was the heir to the glorious political and intellectual traditions of Greece and Rome, and was the capital of the Byzantine Empire, a great power in the eastern Mediterranean until the rise of the Ottomans. So the city's conquest was a huge shock to Christian Europe, and 1453 is a pivotal date in the history of the eastern Mediterranean and of Christian-Muslim relations.

The story of Islam must occupy an important place in the history of the world for any time since the faith began in the seventh century.

The great heritage of classical Islam and of the Arabic-speaking world were deeply affected after 1200 by the Mongol invasions, which disrupted trade routes and devastated Baghdad and other great Muslim cities. Religious quarrels also had intensified. Sunni schools believed the plain words of the Holy Quran, and scholarly agreement about law and custom were all the guidance a good Muslim needed. The Shia[2] believed Islam could only be properly guided by a descendant of the prophet Muhammad, an "imam" or teacher; the Shia mourned the cutting off of the succession of imams in the conflicts of early Islam and hoped in various ways for the coming of a final or hidden imam. They sensed hidden meanings even in the Quran and felt more need for a divinely inspired teacher, preferably an imam, to help them understand it.

Teachings in traditions called Sufi sometimes stayed within Sunni orthodoxy but slipped easily into the Shia path. Islam sets demanding standards of conduct for all believers: daily prayer, a month of fasting from dawn to dark in the month of Ramadan, charity, the pilgrimage to Mecca if possible. But it does not focus much on withdrawal from the world or denial of bodily desires. Still some Muslims on religious quests became full-time wanderers with almost no possessions, engaged in strenuous fasting and all-night prayers, which could lead to stunning moments of union with God and delight in the beauties of his creation. These wanderers were called "Sufis" from the Arabic word for their dark woolen cloaks. They did not violate Muslim rules of conduct but still were viewed with suspicion because they were outside the usual bonds of place, work, and family, and their reports of their experiences seemed to imply that they were closer to God than the ordinary devout householder. They attracted followers among soldiers, craftsmen, and traders, formed organized groups for mutual support, and established lodgings open to all travelers.

The Ottoman Turks were bearers of a Central Asian tradition of political centralization and control of nomads and trade routes that reached its peak in the great Mongol Empire of the 1200s and 1300s. Their language was related to those of the Mongols and other Inner Asian peoples. They were not the first Turks to encroach on the Byzantine Empire; Turks we call Seljuk had won a great victory as early as 1071. The Turks preserved a Central Asian heritage of fluid politics, with frequent violent contests among claimants to a hereditary succession of leadership and the results of such a contest sometimes confirmed by an assembly of warriors. Identities could shift rapidly, as a gifted leadership drew its allies and even its defeated rivals into a new organization with a new name. The Ottomans emerged out of two kinds of interaction within earlier Islamic societies. First, some Turks served as border guards protecting settled areas from other nomads, valuing bravery in battle and the conquest of Islamic and non-Islamic peoples. Second, in towns and along trade routes, traveling merchants spread the teachings of Sufi masters. Sufi teaching centers provided lodging for travelers, and merchants and craftsmen formed brotherhoods of prayer around Sufi teachers. The mystique of brotherhood and response to a holy teacher also drew the fighters from the borders into some of the Sufi brotherhoods. The similarity to the interaction between desert warriors and merchants' networks in the early Arabian stages of the history of Islam is striking.

At first the Ottomans were simply among the more able or lucky of a number of small Turkish principalities on the Byzantine frontiers who brought others loosely under their power; all that was required was that the subordinate ruler lead his forces in a summer campaign under Ottoman command. This process was gradually given formal shape in a system that recognized the right of regional rulers to collect rents from a territory assigned to them, called a *timar*, and their resulting obligation to support certain numbers of cavalry and infantry. After 1300 the Ottomans crossed into Europe, frequently in alliance with one faction or another in Byzantine court politics, and began to elaborate their key strategies for ruling non-Muslims, worked out gradually in the previous centuries in a region where people of many faiths and many languages mingled. These policies made prudent sense in such a region, and also grew out of a basic Muslim respect for Christians and Jews as, like Muslims, "people of the Book," worshippers of the one God, acknowledging many of the same prophets, from Moses and Abraham to Jesus. Muslims saw Christians and Jews as having failed to acknowledge God's last prophet, Muhammad, and his definitive holy book, the Quran, but still worthy of respect. But Christians and Jews were not required to bear arms under a Muslim ruler; instead, they paid an extra head tax.

A second key innovation for the stability of the rising Ottoman state was the creation of full-time paid military forces, called Janissaries from the Turkish words for "new army," who provided more reliable support for the ruler than the warriors who followed regional commanders on a campaign. A third innovation was the devshirme, a requirement that non-Muslim subjects contribute boys to be raised at the Ottoman court as Muslims and slaves of the ruler; devshirme men often rose to positions of great power and trust in the Ottoman state.

After 1400 the Ottomans controlled a large part of the Balkans, with many Christian subjects—Hungarians, Serbs, and others—and there were many signs that living among Christians and intermarrying with them were affecting their cultural life. After the conquest of Constantinople/Istanbul in 1453, the Ottoman rulers were widely accepted in the Muslim world as "sultans," political rulers who upheld Islam, and beginning in the 1540s they claimed that they were caliphs, with full authority in religious matters for Muslims. They also made more formal the status of non-Muslim groups under their own leaders—a Greek patriarch, an Armenian patriarch, a chief rabbi—and allowed them to administer their own laws for their own people, especially in matters of religion, marriage, and inheritance, so that these religious leaders had very considerable political authority.

The Ottomans thus offered all their subjects peace within a wide realm, in which merchants could move about free of robbery and farmers could plant their crops with only minimal fear that they would be devastated by passing armies. It seems that taxes were lighter and more predictable than the exactions of earlier Christian rulers in parts of the Balkans. Churches and synagogues had their places alongside the mosques. Some people must have grieved over the loss of a son to the devshirme, but sometimes a local boy rose high in the Ottoman service and then protected his native place or donated funds for a bridge or other improvement. The general peace and prosperity of the late 1400s was followed by more successful wars, comfortably supported by taxation of growing production. Later, in the 1600s, the consequences of prosperity were more mixed; regional strong men managed to keep control of revenues from their areas and use them to mount challenges to the power of the government in Istanbul. The success of centralized rule over a large area and the continued importance of military power within it have led modern scholars to talk about the Ottomans as one of a number of "gunpowder empires," including the Safavid in Iran and the Mughal in India, greatly dependent on central control of the rapidly improving technology of firearms for the preservation of peace over a wide area.

The Mediterranean in 1500 was not uniformly a sphere of Muslim advance. Far to the west, Islam suffered a setback that had been as long coming as the victory at Istanbul. Muslims had largely ruled the Iberian Peninsula (modern Spain and Portugal) for centuries, and under them it had a vibrant culture and rich arts, with a large degree of toleration of Christians and Jews. But Christian knights pushing out of the north had conquered most of the peninsula by about 1300, and only the small kingdom of Granada in the far south offered any real resistance. It fell to Christian forces in January 1492. The Christian monarchs were far less tolerant than the Muslims had been; Jews and Muslims were required to convert or leave. A substantial number of Iberian Jews resettled in Istanbul. A naval victory by a Christian coalition at Lepanto off the coast of Greece in 1571 ended the threat of a growing Ottoman naval power, but the Ottomans remained largely in control of the eastern Mediterranean, facing French and Spanish naval power in the waters around Italy and farther west.

From 1510 to 1520, the Ottoman Empire stood in great power and prosperity at a moment of plural possibilities opened up by its own position at the crossroads of Eurasia and by the big changes in the maritime world set off by the voyages of Columbus and Vasco da Gama. It faced two hostile powers, the Mamluk sultans in Egypt whose power reached up into modern Syria, and the new, militantly Shia Safavid state in Iran. Both had drawn tax revenues from maritime trade, up the Persian Gulf and up the Red Sea, that was now being at least temporarily disrupted by the attacks of the Portuguese in the Indian Ocean. When a great Ottoman army set out toward Syria in 1516, it was not clear which way it would go. When the army turned toward Egypt, many Syrian power-holders came over to the Ottoman side, and by the end of 1517, Mamluk power was extinguished and Egypt was securely under Ottoman control. Other territorial gains followed: In 1534 the Ottomans took Baghdad and most of Iraq from the Iranian Safavids, the beginning of a hundred years of confrontation on that frontier. In the Balkans a brief siege of Vienna in 1529 was followed by many years of back-and-forth warfare over Hungary and Serbia. And although the Ottomans had no tradition of warfare at sea, they now developed a formidable presence in the Mediterranean, taking Cyprus in 1570–71 and establishing a semi-autonomous outpost far to the west, at Algiers, in 1517.

Thus the Ottomans had far more territory under their control, including far more Christians. In Shia Persia they confronted a really serious challenge to their Sunni Islam and their strategic dominance in the region. Holding the many-sided empire together and keeping it on the straight and narrow would require a great deal of institutional development. The reign of the great Suleyman "the lawgiver" or "the legislator," from 1520 to 1566 is generally thought to be the peak of the Ottoman political achievement. They developed law codes and regular bureaucratic structures. They tried to limit Shia and Sufi practices and to impose Sunni orthodoxy. A special worry was the participation of

A simply dressed pilgrim to the shrines of Mashhad, Iran, in 1598 removes his turban and scratches his head in weariness or puzzlement. Pilgrimages to the tombs of great teachers were a special feature of Shia Islam. Freer Gallery of Art, Smithsonian Institution, Washington, DC: Purchase, F1953.12.

city-dwellers, including soldiers, in the meetings of "dervish" orders that followed the teaching of some Sufi master; these events often included much singing and ecstatic dancing, quite a change from the austere bowing and reciting of the daily Muslim prayers.

The strengthening of Ottoman ties to the world of Islam was a direct result of their conquests. The Sharifs, the guardians of the holy cities of Mecca and Medina, the sites of the origins of Islam, gave their allegiance to the Ottomans, and thus they could be appointed and removed by Istanbul. This meant that the great annual caravans of pilgrims from Damascus and Cairo now were under Ottoman protection and supervision. Troops guarded each caravan and garrisoned outposts along the caravan routes. Bigger expeditions might be launched to push back nomadic raiders that threatened the caravan routes, or the raiders might be simply paid to stay away. Shia pilgrims from Iran could not be kept away entirely, but they were required to come the long way around via Damascus and were subjected to much obstruction and verbal abuse in the holy cities.

It would be hard to overestimate the importance of the holy cities and of the Hajj, the great annual pilgrimage, in the world of Islam in early modern times. This gave Islam its integrity amid all its diversity of peoples, from Southeast Asia to China to West Africa. Everywhere Muslims turned in prayer toward Mecca, and when they came on pilgrimage encountered many preachers of renewal and return to fundamentals, saw the places where the prophet had received God's last word, and vowed to follow the pure Islamic way they experienced there. The Hajj was a religious duty for every Muslim who was physically and financially able to make the trip. It culminated in great ceremonies on a few days during one month. Since the Islamic calendar consists of twelve lunar months, the solar calendar timing of the Hajj changed from year to year, posing different problems for pilgrims coming across the deserts at the peak of the summer heat or needing to sail from India to the Red Sea when the winds were blowing in the right direction. Pilgrims might have to wait for months at some halfway point, or in Mecca and Medina after the conclusion of the ceremonies. Frequently they brought along spices, fabrics, and incense woods from their home countries to sell and pay the expenses of the trip. Not inappropriately for a faith that had its origins in revelations to a merchant and first converts from communities of merchants, the Hajj became a great pump of early modern world trade. On the Hajj the individual pilgrim donned plain white garments that removed all distinctions of wealth or national origin. Each individual pilgrim was walking and running where prophets from Abraham onward had walked and run. They circled the Ka'aba, the cubic building of black stone in the square of the Great Mosque, and struggled through the crowds to get a chance to touch it, praying and weeping. They ran back and forth between the two wells as Hagar had done searching for water for her son, Ishmael. On the final day they went outside Mecca to the Plain of Arafat and prayed fervently for forgiveness for their sins.

There were many stories of people who had changed their lives after these experiences. Even if they were already pious or still a bit cynical afterward, all now bore the title of "Hajji" and were given special respect in any Muslim community. Many movements of renewal and purification across the Islamic world got their start with a returning pilgrim's determination to bring to his own people the pure and intense Islam he or she had experienced. This was a more effective strategy for defending a religious tradition from change and corruption than the bureaucratic and authoritarian enforcement of orthodoxy to which the Roman Catholic Church devoted so much effort in these centuries.

In the 1600s the Ottoman Empire still was a great power, and Istanbul was one of the world's largest cities, rich in all kinds of luxury goods, offering much work to architects, painters, and craftsmen from all over the Islamic world and even from Christian Europe. A particularly civilized feature of its urban life was the coffee house; coffee, originating in Ethiopia and Yemen, had spread widely through the Islamic world, all the more because good Muslims abstained from alcohol. There was a rich variety of poetry and other literature, some of it written by the sultans themselves, in Ottoman Turkish and in Persian. In addition to the established presence of Christian and Jewish communities, there were many different branches and tendencies within Islam. Medieval Muslims had done much to preserve Greek science and philosophy through preceding centuries, but many Muslims were suspicious of non-Islamic learning, especially translations of the Greeks, and over time their influence grew.

A final odd feature of Ottoman cultural life was that no printing in Arabic or in Ottoman Turkish existed in the Ottoman realm until well after 1700. The rulers knew about printing; Greeks, Armenians, and Jews all had presses in Istanbul. But the hand-copying of sacred texts had great prestige in Islam, and the Ottomans understood that in Christian Europe the printing of religious arguments had contributed to just the kind of conflict among believers they dreaded in their own realms. Catholics and Protestants were doing some printing in Arabic in Christian Europe in their efforts to win the allegiance of the Christians of what is now Lebanon, then part of the Ottoman Empire; this was just the kind of stirring up of ethno-religious tension that could make the multi-ethnic and multi-religious empire harder to govern.

Ottoman politics in the 1600s was a nasty business. Several sultans were deposed and killed by the Janissaries. But the war machine still was formidable. It took Crete as late as 1669 and besieged Vienna in 1683. The devshirme system was largely abandoned, but it made a final contribution to Ottoman survival; the administration of the empire for much of the 1600s was in the hands of a succession of chief ministers from one family of Albanian devshirme origin. The defeat of the Ottoman armies before Vienna in 1683 led to years of chaos on the great plains of southeastern Europe, including rebellions by unpaid Ottoman troops who then marched on Istanbul. By 1700 the empire seemed to have pulled back from the brink of chaos, but remained fragile.

The multiple minarets of the Grand Mosque in Mecca and the black cubic Ka'aba in its open square are the central images in an Ottoman ceramic plaque from the 1600s. Every good Muslim hoped to see them with his or her own eyes while on the Hajj pilgrimage. Réunion des Musées Nationaux / Art Resource, NY.

The Safavid Empire of Iran originated in developments not very different from the Ottoman beginnings, with the growth of Sufi brotherhoods and networks among border warriors and urban merchants. Sufi teachings could be kept in the bounds of Sunni Islam, but there always was tension. The mix with Shia concepts of hidden teachers and meanings, of messianic hopes for the future, was much less tense and more powerful.

The Safavid order began in the 1300s as a Sufi movement, strong among border soldiers and urban merchants and craftsmen. It turned political after 1450, and from 1499 to 1501 found an inspired leader, Ismail, who claimed powers of prophecy and led his armies to conquer the city of Tabriz, where he was proclaimed shah. His forces conquered all of Persia (now Iran) in about ten years, and he ruled until he died in 1524. Ismail, quite a long way from Islamic orthodoxy, claimed that he was the reincarnation of Adam, Noah, Abraham, Moses, Jesus, Muhammad, and Alexander the Great. He is reported to have proclaimed:

> "In me is Prophethood and the mystery of Holiness.
> I am God's Eye; come now, oh blind man gone astray, to behold
> the truth that I am the Absolute Doer of whom they speak.
> Sun and Moon are in my power."[3]

In the 1500s the Safavids shaped a new world of Shia culture and religion in Iran,[4] which remains the foundation of Iranian life and of the lives of Shia elsewhere, as in Iraq, to this day. At certain times in the Muslim calendar, Shia cities were and still are full of dramatic presentations of the martyrdom of the last true imam and of processions of men mourning his death and celebrating his sacrifice for the people of Islam. Many Shia were and are devoted followers of one or another imam, a teacher of special religious power and insight.

At the beginning many Iranians were Sunni, and it seems that many conversions to Shia allegiance were forced. But forced conversion produces long-term results only when the coercion touches something ready for change. Perhaps Iranians found in Shia belief and practices that enabled them to believe themselves better Muslims than the Arab enemies to the west. Perhaps Iran's pre-Islamic belief in god-kings was echoed in Safavid exaltation of the role of the monarch. Safavid Shahs were thought to have special access to God. So were the great imams, some of whom became too dangerous to the rulers and were eliminated.

Beginning under Ismail's son Tahmasp, the shah delegated much of his religious authority to properly controlled imams. A magnificent urban culture took shape, especially in the splendid new buildings of Isfahan, under the great Shah Abbas, 1588–1629. Production and export of silk brought Safavid Iran into the interconnected world of trade. The long struggle with the Ottomans ended in 1639. In the late 1600s Iran was suffering from internal disorders, and its vibrant, tension-filled culture seems to have been giving way to a Shia orthodoxy that had long forgotten Ismail's claims of near-divinity and in which great imams had immense authority.

The Safavid Empire had risen in struggle with its Timurid neighbor to the northeast, in what are now the republics of Kazakhstan and Uzbekistan. The name Timur still carried weight in 1450, although Timur, the last great warrior of the Mongol tradition, died on his way

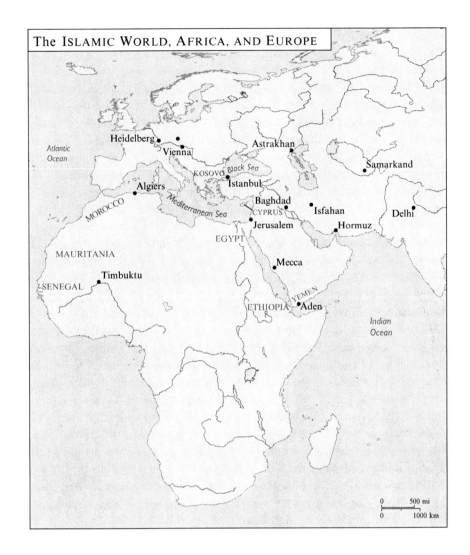

Atlantic
Ocean

Heidelberg
Vienna
Astrakhan
Samarkand
KOSOVO
Black Sea
Caspian Sea
Algiers
Istanbul
MOROCCO
Mediterranean Sea
Baghdad
CYPRUS
Isfahan
Delhi
Jerusalem
Hormuz
EGYPT
MAURITANIA
Mecca
SENEGAL
Timbuktu
ETHIOPIA
YEMEN
Aden
Indian
Ocean

0   500 mi
0   1000 km

to invade China in 1405. Stories of him passed into the literatures of many peoples; there is even the well-known play, "Tamerlane," by Christopher Marlowe, a contemporary of Shakespeare. In the eyes of many Iranians, the nomads on their northeastern frontier were everything wild and uncouth. But the Mongol rule had imposed a kind of peace that made it possible for caravans to move along the Silk Road in safety, and the Mongols also had been interested in learning from the high cultures of all the peoples they ruled. Some of Timur's heirs, especially his grandson Ulugh Beg, did not deserve the Iranian put-downs of their culture and intellect. Ulugh Beg ruled in semi-independence from his relatives at Samarkand from 1409 to his death in 1449. He was a terrible general, always dithering and changing his plans. But he was a great patron of the arts, and he ordered the building of magnificent schools, gardens, baths, and gates at Samarkand and Bukhara, some of which still can be seen. His passion for knowledge of the natural world led him to build an observatory and assemble more than sixty scientists to design other instruments and to record observations. The star tables they compiled were repeatedly copied and translated; a Latin translation was published in England as late as 1652. After Ulugh Beg died, his successors did not keep up the work, but his scientists found employment at other courts of the Muslim world.

The vibrant world of Samarkand, Bukhara, and, a little later, Kabul looked both ways, to the great culture of Iran and to the riches of the Indian subcontinent. The third of the great Muslim "gunpowder empires" was the Mughal, in what is now India and Pakistan. The Muslim encounter with Hinduism was across a gulf of approaches to religion that seemed almost unbridgeable, far wider than in the encounters with Christianity. Muslims, who recognized only one supreme and unrepresentable God and viewed all portrayals of human and animal forms as usurpations of the powers of the creator, shuddered at the wild profusion of the Hindu imagination, with its gods and goddesses with many arms or animal heads. Muslims did not eat pork but enjoyed slaughtering and eating an ox, an animal sacred to the Hindus. But Hindus had been living under Muslim rulers in parts of northern India plain since the eleventh century. Even among themselves, Hindus lived in separate groups by rank and occupation, which we sometimes call castes. Castes did not intermarry and had only carefully regulated contact with each other; it was not too much of a stretch for Hindus to develop new rules for getting along with the Muslims in their midst.

The Mughals came down out of what now is Afghanistan, heirs of the great Mongol tradition by way of the descendants of Timur. They first conquered Delhi and Agra on the north Indian plain in 1526, but then were beaten back by rival invaders from the north and came to stay only in the 1550s. The first Mughal conqueror of the north Indian plain, Babur, has left us a long and richly observant autobiography, full of details of the intrigues and family connections of the rulers of Inner Asia, but also of details of Samarkand, Kabul, and other cities, their fine buildings, the farms irrigated by summer runoff waters from the great mountains, their snowy peaks often in sight, producing the melons, grapes, apples, and other fruits that Babur recalled in fond detail. He was fascinated by the north Indian plain, but it is clear that he was homesick for Kabul: "Most of the provinces...are located on flat terrain. So many cities and so many provinces—yet there is no running water anywhere....Hindustan is a place of little charm. There is no beauty in its people, no graceful social intercourse, no poetic talent or understanding, no etiquette, nobility, or manliness. The arts and crafts have no harmony or symmetry. There are no good horses, meat, grapes, melons, or other fruit. There is no ice, cold water, good food or bread in the markets. There are no baths and no madrasas [Islamic schools]."[5]

The energy and effectiveness of the Mughal rulers peaked early, under the Emperor Akbar, who ruled from 1556 to 1605. He defeated and co-opted the Hindu Rajput warriors of the deserts of what is now the state of Rajasthan, giving them high commands in his centralized armies. In the Rajput version of Hindu belief and practice, bravery and loyalty in warfare were primary values, and the Rajputs responded to Mughal appointment to military commands not only with loyal service but by permitting their daughters to marry Mughal princes. Akbar also brought in many Iranian specialists in taxation and record-keeping to help him in his efforts to get full control of the riches of his realm. When he launched an effort to document and control the tax revenues of his realm, he put a Hindu minister in charge. The Mughals' very large army was supposed to be paid out of central tax revenues, but compromises with local powerbrokers always were necessary, and in many areas the rulers had to settle for much less than full control.

The Mughals were heirs of a Turkish and Mongol Central Asian tradition in which strong women sometimes played major political roles when their husbands were away on campaign or with the herds. At the Mughal court, senior women, especially wives and mothers of the emperors, were powerful and respected advisors. In the reign of Akbar, a large party of palace women went on the pilgrimage to Mecca, staying away for more than three years.

Akbar had wide-ranging interests. Some of the marvelous buildings that housed his court still stand at Delhi, Agra, and Fatehpur Sikri. The style owes much to Iranian architecture. Italian artisans did some of the finest stone inlay work. Much court literature was in the Persian language, and Iranian examples inspired a fine tradition of miniature painting. Akbar particularly enjoyed hearing the representatives of various religions debate their beliefs—Sunnis, Shia, Sufis, Hindus of every kind, and even Christians, including Jesuit missionaries from Portugal and Italy. To him, several lineages of Sufi masters whose quests for union with God seemed to bridge the impossible gulf between Hinduism and Islam. Late in his life he experimented with a full-scale synthetic new religion with himself as the prophet, to the growing horror of more orthodox Muslims.

Under the rules of Akbar's son Jahangir (ruled 1605–1627) and grandson Shah Jahan (ruled 1628–1658), the empire continued to expand on all its frontiers and to consolidate power internally. Advances to the south brought large populations with their own languages and distinctive forms of Hinduism, and some ports under Mughal rule. Several areas of the empire were major centers of production of cotton and silk textiles that were exported to Southeast Asia, the Middle East, and increasingly to Europe. Most of the empire's tax revenues went to support its armies, and military command and achievement remained keys to wealth and power. Rulers at all levels built lavishly at their capitals and at Hindu and Muslim centers of pilgrimage; the Taj Mahal is the tomb Shah Jahan built for his favorite wife and himself. But serious Muslims remained unimpressed by all the worldly beauty. They were most uncomfortable with the Hindu "idolatry" they saw all around them and with the deviations from Muslim orthodoxy that some of the popular Sufi orders adopted, clearly a result of interaction with Hinduism. At the end of Shah Jahan's reign, a savage civil war exploded among his adult sons. One of them, Dara Shukoh, was a wide-ranging religious enthusiast who saw similarities in Sufi and Hindu teachings. Another was Aurangzeb, an austerely devout and narrow Muslim. Aurangzeb won, and he ruled until 1707.

Akbar had abolished the head tax required of non-Muslim subjects; Aurangzeb brought it back in 1679, to widespread protest. He made lavish grants for the building of new mosques, and some recently built or repaired Hindu temples were torn down. In western India, a time bomb of Hindu resentment was ticking, as Shivaji, a local ruler of the Maratha people, built up his power in areas where the Mughals could not control him. He killed a Muslim general in 1657, made an uneasy peace with the Mughal court and then broke the peace and fled from the court, and in 1674 had himself crowned as an independent Hindu king. His fast-moving cavalry raiders kept the Mughals off balance, and his proclamations attacking Aurangzeb's anti-Hindu policies won much sympathy. He died in 1680, but the Maratha power continued to grow under his son and other leaders. After 1700 regional power centers within the Mughal empire, especially Bengal, and several Maratha kingdoms pulled away from the Mughal center, and the British and the French learned how to fish in the troubled waters of Mughal decline.

The Ottomans, Safavids, and Mughals all were conquerors. After 1450 the warrior side of the Islamic tradition was by no means dead; in

Islam a central value is jihad, or striving, which can mean moral striving for a better society or for individual integrity but certainly often has meant an armed struggle. In the 1500s and 1600s, however, most of the geographic expansion of the world of Islam was the work of merchants. This was especially true in maritime Southeast Asia (roughly modern Malaysia and Indonesia) and in west Africa south of the Sahara. Islam is perhaps the most portable of the great religions, keeping its base in the reading of the Quran in Arabic, maintaining a flow of pilgrims to a sacred center, and respecting common traditions of law so that a merchant, religious teacher, or legal expert could move around anywhere in the Muslim world and know pretty well what the rules were. (Jews kept their language and law, but had limited chances to return to Jerusalem and had limited interest in converting the people among whom they lived; Christians had many laws, many languages, and many tangles of church authority.) And although a new outpost of Islam always would be affected by the non-Muslim culture around it, local people, even rulers, found it fairly easy to convert, and teachers coming from the Muslim heartlands and pilgrims returning from Mecca would regularly agitate for a purer Islamic way of life.

In maritime Southeast Asia, Muslim merchants came from India and occasionally from Persia and the Arab lands. On the north coast of Java and even in southern Vietnam, graves with Muslim inscriptions and other artifacts provide evidence of Muslim settlement before 1450. The most important early center of Islam in Southeast Asia was the city-state of Melaka (previously spelled Malacca) on the Malay Peninsula, facing Sumatra across the Strait of Melaka; earlier centers of trade had been further south on the Sumatra side. Melaka had strong connections with the Chinese trading network in the region. According to one tradition, Melaka's folk hero was taught to recite the Quran by a trader from India. The rulers of Melaka were Muslim, claiming the special honors due to protectors of the religion, before 1450.

Islam was far out in the eastern islands, including Mindanao in the modern Philippines, before the Europeans arrived there. Portuguese hostility contributed greatly to its further spread. After the Portuguese conquered Melaka in 1511, the former rulers moved down the coast to Johor near modern Singapore and sought allies in a series of unsuccessful counterattacks. The most important of these allies was Aceh[6] on the northern tip of Sumatra, which became the most Muslim and one of the most powerful trading states in Southeast Asia, reaching a peak of prosperity under its great ruler Iskander Muda between 1607 and 1636. Banten near the west end of Java was another Muslim trading state from the mid-1500s until the Dutch conquered it and shut it down in 1682. On the island of Sulawesi, the rulers of the kingdom of Makassar converted to Islam in 1605. Here as elsewhere rulers seeking allies against the Portuguese, and the appeal of Sufi teachings and teachers, aided the efforts of Muslim merchants.

The Mediterranean was Christian on most of its north side, Muslim on the south and east, but all sides had big cities dependent on maritime trade, fertile valleys with little or no summer rain, and shepherds moving flocks between winter and summer pastures.[7] There was a great deal of trade, despite the heritages of hostility. European Catholics and Protestants lived and traded at Istanbul on the same terms as other "peoples of the Book." Italian merchants came to Cairo and Alexandria to buy the spices and other luxury goods that arrived by way of the Red Sea; Portuguese attacks in the Indian Ocean set back this commerce after 1498, but it soon revived.

There was a lot of nasty conflict. The Spanish monarchy made several attempts to establish a fortified naval base on the southern side of the Mediterranean, none of which accomplished much except to exhaust Spanish budgets and reinforce Muslim grievances. The most persistent form of revenge was "piracy," attacking ships at sea, seizing their goods, and taking their crews captive. Captives with rich relatives might be ransomed; the others would be enslaved, the men pulling an oar in a galley, the women serving in a household or harem. To European Christians this marauding was a key example of Muslim savagery, with Algiers as the great center of marauding and of European efforts to free slaves. By the late 1600s local leaders at Algiers had reduced Ottoman control to forms and vestiges, and the assertive French monarchy was regularly attacking Algiers. The first foreign venture of the new United States was to the "shores of Tripoli" against the "Barbary pirates." But the Europeans also took and enslaved captives and demanded ransom. Near the great Doge's Palace in Venice is the "Riva degli Schiavoni," the "Slaves' Quay," where many of them landed.

Islam was present on the trade routes along the southern fringe of the Sahara long before 1450. Some trade moved along the Niger River, one route reached down to the Asante gold fields in the north of modern Ghana, and caravan routes carried gold and other goods across the Sahara to the southern shore of the Mediterranean. King Mansa Musa of Mali had made his pilgrimage to Mecca in 1325, dazzling the sophisticated, wealthy people of Cairo with his splendid procession and lavish distribution of gold. After 1468 Timbuktu on the Niger emerged under the rule of the kingdom of Songhay as a great center of trade and of

Islamic learning. In 1496 and 1497 King Askia Muhammad of Songhay went on his pilgrimage to Mecca. The Muslim kingdom of Borno was at a peak of commercial and military power in the early 1600s. By that time, however, the effects of the Portuguese along the coasts were being felt. Some gold now was shipped south from Asante to the Portuguese Elmina Castle. A war set off by Portuguese attacks in Morocco seems to have contributed to a Moroccan invasion across the Sahara in 1591, which destabilized the region along the Niger for many years.

Elsewhere, people wanting to pursue a fully Islamic way of life and avoid connection with non-Muslim customs and beliefs withdrew into separate communities, which often were centers of trade because of connections of trust and common law among Muslims. In the region of modern Senegal, some time before 1650, the followers of a teacher named Salimu Sware explicitly rejected the Islamic warrior tradition, insisting that jihad, striving, meant only spiritual striving. After the decline and violence that began around 1600, scholars in Timbuktu and the surrounding area hid Islamic manuscripts or showed them only to selected circles of students. Four centuries later, an international effort is under way to find, catalogue, and preserve them.

So Islam, with its principles of tolerance for other "peoples of the Book" and its strategies for living among other people and maintaining its own integrity, had done much to link peoples from Senegal to Serbia to Melaka. But by 1700 the Muslim world was on the defensive, less open to ideas from outside, facing European aggression from the Balkans to India and the Spice Islands, its networks of connections across Asia losing market share to the European networks of maritime connections.

CHAPTER 2

Columbian Exchanges, 1490–1530

"Tierra! Tierra!" "Land! Land!" The ships had been at sea for thirty-seven days, sailing straight west into the unknown. The crew had grown very uneasy, then relaxed a bit as they saw in the water a few tree branches and other signs of land nearby. On the night of October 11 they thought they had seen fires on the horizon. As the three little ships anchored near the low, wooded shore, local people gathered to look at them. Already inclined, as a result of unfriendly encounters with Africans, to take bare brown skin as a sign of savagery, the Europeans did not hesitate to go ashore and proclaim the sovereignty of their king and queen, Ferdinand and Isabella of Spain.

It was the morning of October 12, 1492, one of the most famous and controversial dates in world history. "Columbus's discovery of America" is the conventional description. But the people on shore, and the native peoples all up and down the Americas, knew where they were and who their neighbors were, and had no need to be discovered. For Columbus and his captains and sailors, there was no question that "discovery" was the right word. They had found something new, but they were not sure what it was. In trying to understand their discoveries, they drew on the Christian faith, Biblical texts, ancient texts in Greek and Latin, and the realities of trade in their own times: precious spices from Southeast Asian islands, gold from tropical West Africa, and the power and wealth of China. Columbus, hoping he was somewhere near the spice islands and other riches of the Indian Ocean, called the islands he found the Indies—we still call them the West Indies—and the native people Indians. If he had had to seek the permission of powerful rulers to trade or even to anchor, as the Portuguese did in West Africa, he might have settled for a trading post dependent on a local ruler.

But the Taino people had neither the centralized political organization nor the weapons to mount a sustained resistance. Soon, on the larger island that now is occupied by Haiti and the Dominican Republic, Columbus founded a small Spanish city and began treating the Taino as subjects of the Spanish crown. His efforts to impose a tax in gold on them produced meager results. He enslaved some captives taken in small battles and began to think about a trade in slaves, as in Africa, as a source of profit.

Accepting slavery but still deeply religious, Columbus was horrified by the behavior of his Spanish colonists, many of them ex-convicts, who expected to live off plunder and extortion from the Taino and often defied the colony's leaders. By the time he died in 1506, the Spanish had founded more cities and many more settlers had come, but his tiny colony was so near complete breakdown that the whole amazing adventure could have disappeared in mutual slaughter, with a few survivors going native.

It did not. Columbus's arrival was the beginning of a huge transformation and disaster for the native peoples of the Americas. The disaster was not entirely the result of Spanish malevolence, although there were plenty of greed, slave-hunting, and a few episodes of deliberate genocide. European pigs and cattle running wild gave the native people of the Americas easier access to meat than they had previously, but the animals trashed many of their gardens. Europeans learned about and took to other parts of the world some major food crops—potatoes, yams, tomatoes, chili peppers, and maize (corn)- and one very attractive non-food crop, tobacco. Other exchanges soon developed, of silver, of religion, of horses as in Texas, and of people settling and mixing their genes and their cultures.

European-borne diseases, especially measles and smallpox, wreaked the worst havoc in the Americas, because the natives had no resistance to them. This was the result of a "Columbian exchange" of biological organisms that had evolved in different directions in the twenty thousand years or more when there had been very little contact between Eurasia and the Americas. Beginning around 1520 in Mexico we have eyewitness accounts of thousands dying in the agonies of smallpox. For the islands, it is hard to sort out the effects of disease, overwork, and deliberate slaughter. The natives of the Bahamas were wiped out, and those of Cuba were almost decimated. Vivid denunciations of the Cuba quasi-holocaust by the Dominican preacher Bartolomé de Las Casas, on the spot and then at the royal court in Spain, set off complicated debates and a long struggle to formulate policies that would salve consciences but preserve conquests. Decade after decade until after 1800, the diseases reached new isolated groups of non-immune native people, and the horrors began all over again. Just in the first century of contact, the native population of the Americas fell to less than 10 percent of pre-contact numbers and possibly to 3 percent.

Columbus's troubles in the islands were not the end of his discoveries. On his third voyage, from 1498 to 1500, Columbus had realized that fresh water far offshore from the mouth of the Orinoco River could only come from a great river on a great land mass: "I believe that this is a very great continent, until today unknown....And further I am supported by the saying of many Carib Indians whom I took at other times, who said that to the south of them there was mainland...and they said that in it there was much gold."[1] On his fourth voyage he had touched the Central American coast. There was a continent there, and it was not Asia. In 1517, as the conquest of Cuba wound down, an expedition reached the Yucatán Peninsula. The explorers were astonished to find large stone buildings and warriors in padded cotton armor wearing a few gold ornaments. These were the Maya, no longer building great pyramids but preserving much of one of the oldest and most sophisticated cultures of the Americas. The Spanish were not interested in learning about other cultures, but they thought the stonework suggested a rich empire somewhere inland, and above all they saw the gold. They thought the warriors, dangerous and alien as they seemed on first meeting, would not stand a chance against a few hundred Spaniards with steel armor, firearms, and horses.

The Spanish-Maya interaction continued, but the first great drama on the American mainland was the meeting of the Spanish and the Aztecs from 1519 to 1521. It is the greatest story in human history of encounter between two groups who only can see each other as utterly alien intelligent beings. The Spanish were awed by the size and beauty of the great Aztec capital, Tenochtitlán, where Mexico City now stands, and horrified by the human sacrifices that the Aztecs believed were necessary for keeping the sun moving on its daily course across the sky. To the Aztecs, the Spanish ships were weird mountains riding out on the sea, their horses some kind of strange deer, their clanking iron armor uncanny and impenetrable by the Aztecs' arrows, their firearms and even their crossbows lethal at a distance. The Aztecs probably did not see the Spanish as gods, as some old texts suggested, but they found them menacing and incomprehensible.

The Aztecs were the last in a sequence of great temple-building powers in the Valley of Mexico. As they rose to dominate the area in the mid-1400s, they added their own hummingbird god to the older gods worshipped by other peoples in the valley. Captives taken in war, including some very stylized "battles" with nearby allies, were sacrificed to the gods on the great pyramids.

Hernán Cortés was a fairly typical product of the Christian reconquest of Spain from the Muslims and of the rape of the West Indies, a brilliant and completely ruthless improviser. When his forces landed in April 1519 near modern Vera Cruz with about six hundred men, he formed a town government, as often had been done in areas conquered from the Muslims in Spain, to consolidate his own independent authority. He soon sensed that resentment of Aztec power on the edges of their empire would give him many Native American allies. In August his men fought some small battles with the people of Tlaxcala, who then came over to his side. As he advanced inland the Aztecs sought to resist, but found they could do little against the iron armor, the firearms, and the lancers on horseback. When they arrived at Tenochtitlán in November, the Aztec ruler, Moctezuma, was ready to treat them as dangerous guests, and ordered that they be given food and lodging. He could not risk battle in an open field, even if he could assemble more than ten thousand men against Cortés's five or six hundred; even if his men killed every Spaniard, so many Aztecs would be killed that it would destroy his authority and open the way for attacks by his enemies.

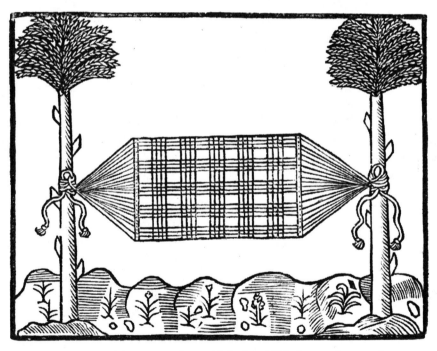

A Spanish history of the West Indies published in 1535 shows a hammock, unknown to Europeans before they came to the Caribbean and South America. The text comments that "they are good, clean beds." (Son buenas camas y limpias.) Library of Congress.

When a new force of Spanish ships and soldiers arrived at Vera Cruz in April 1520, it seemed likely that they had been sent to bring Cortés under control. But Cortés put Moctezuma under arrest in his own capital, marched to the coast, and convinced the newly arrived Spaniards that he was in control of the situation; so that they joined his forces. The Aztecs tried to admit and trap this larger force, but on the Noche Triste, "Night of Sorrow," at the end of June, the Spaniards fought their way out, retreated to the coast, and killed Moctezuma. Now they found far more Native American allies, especially the people of Texcoco, and with their numbers and the superiority of their own military technology fought their way to complete, permanent victory and occupation of Tenochtitlán by August 1521. The Spanish leveled the great pyramids and palaces, and laid the foundations for a Spanish city, today's Mexico City.

One of Cortés's soldiers, Bernal Díaz del Castillo, later wrote: "When we saw so many cities and villages built in the water and other great towns on dry land, we were amazed and said that is was like the enchantments they tell of in the legend of Amadis [one of the tales of chivalry so popular in those times], on account of the great towers...and buildings rising from the water....Of these wonders that I then beheld today all is overthrown and lost, nothing left standing."[2]

Other Spaniards were not slow to try to follow the splendid example of Cortés. Francisco Pizarro carefully investigated the Pacific coast south of Panama, went to Spain with evidence of a rich kingdom there, and obtained the king's consent that he would govern whatever he conquered. Several of his brothers, as well as an excellent organizer named Diego de Almagro, joined him. Landing on the coast of modern Peru in 1532, Pizarro marched into the mountains with fewer than two hundred men.

The Inca Empire Pizarro was invading had grown up about a hundred years earlier, the latest of several empires in the singular ecology and economics of the Andes. It had a better food supply at high elevations than anywhere else in the world, because this area was home of the potato, the Americas' greatest gift to Eurasia in the Columbian Exchange. The local people had developed many varieties of the vegetable and techniques for freeze-drying it in the cold, thin air, providing a reliable year-round food supply. The Andean peoples had other resources: the fine wool of the llamas and alpacas, other food crops at lower elevations, and even salt and dried fish from the coast. Local communities assured themselves of supplies of these commodities by sending members to live and work in each zone, from sea level to high in the mountains.

Ruling elites had learned how to turn this system to their own advantage, requiring each community to send people to work for them, and keeping track of goods and people by *quipu*, knotted cords that recorded numbers of supplies collected or people on a work party. The Inca, expanding on the work of earlier empires, had extended their rule farther, building roads of fitted stone blocks and putting garrisons in outpost forts, and thus required people to go farther from home for longer times on these work assignments. This was nothing like the horror subject peoples endured when they had to provide captives to the Aztecs for sacrifice, but they resented the burdens; as a result some people stayed neutral or even joined with the Spanish.

And all the subject peoples were accustomed to being part of an empire; the habit of submission to central authority, and the system of roads and garrisons that reinforced it, also would aid Spanish expansion. In Cuzco, Peru, which was the Inca capital, we still can see the magnificent stonework of their temples to the sun and to the ancestors. But the large amounts of magnificently worked gold, silver, and copper that adorned temples and palaces, that so attracted the Spanish are long gone.

Pizarro marched his little force inland and somehow obtained a personal meeting with the Inca ruler Atahualpa in a town square. The Spaniards used their firearms in a devastating ambush, killing several thousand of the Inca soldiers and taking Atahualpa prisoner. Atahualpa tried to buy his freedom from his greedy captors by giving them enough gold to fill the room he was standing in up to his outstretched arms and the next two rooms with silver measured the same way. Pizarro accepted, the Incas delivered the gold and silver, and Pizarro killed Atahualpa anyway. The Spanish now rapidly took control of the headless empire. There was resistance; in 1536 forces led by a brother of the dead ruler almost drove them out.

By the mid-1540s Spanish power reached from modern Ecuador to central Chile. But what was Spanish power? Pizarro left Pedro de Almagro out of the division of the spoils, Almagro rebelled and was killed, and Almagro's son had Pizarro assassinated. Francisco Pizarro's brother Gonzalo tried to take control, but both sides were tired of the fighting and by 1548 lawyers and officials sent from Spain were getting a grip on the situation.

By 1580 or 1600 the results of these epics of greed, slaughter, and misery were somewhat surprising. A fair number of Spaniards lived in comfort on estates or in colonial cities; others took their wealth back to Spain. The great conquistadores did not turn their plunder into independent power bases. In the Andes the Pizarros and their enemies largely eliminated each other. Cortés went to Spain and got royal support against his enemies, but settled for vast land-holdings and limited political power. Mexico City and Lima became the seats of viceroys, usually from the high Spanish nobility, who lived in great splendor and had wide administrative powers. More important for steady Spanish control over these vast realms was the creation from 1531 on, in Mexico City, Lima, and nine regional capitals, of *audiencias*. These courts of law gradually took on more and more administrative duties and often sent individual judges on tours of inspection and adjudication in outlying areas. The judges, university-trained lawyers from Spain, took their time and frequently gave way to local pressure, but they gradually built up structures of precedent and authority to which local people appealed in their disputes with each other. Large-scale organized violence was extremely rare in areas under full Spanish administration from 1550 to 1700.

The kings of Spain got what they wanted from the Americas: immense quantities of silver and smaller amounts of gold to support their efforts to dominate the politics of Europe and crush the new Protestant menace. The most spectacular mine was the "mountain of silver" at Potosí in modern Bolivia, which around 1600 was pouring unprecedented quantities of silver into the world system. Mines in the highlands of Mexico eventually equaled or surpassed Potosí's production. The general inflation that accompanied commercial growth and made trouble for government finances in Europe in the late 1500s owed something to the inflow of silver, and also something to improving banking and credit systems. The flow of silver became less steady and reliable in the mid-1600s. Quite a lot of the silver flowed on through Europe toward Asia, especially China, to buy Chinese silks, lacquer, and porcelain. The kings of Spain took as tax one fifth of all silver mined in their American realms.

The flow of silver may actually have hampered Spanish responses to the great changes of the times, giving the rulers a sense that they did not need to make their government more efficient or their economy more productive, since they could get their way by paying big armies and bribing rulers and elites. Their efforts to invade England in 1588 and to suppress revolt in the Netherlands, and to support Catholic rulers against Protestant in Germany, from the 1580s to 1648, all failed. The silver that flowed through private Spanish hands mostly went on elsewhere in Europe or Asia to pay for imported luxury goods and did little to support Spanish agriculture or craft production. By 1650 Spain was the sick man of Europe, badly governed, poor, and plagued by bandits.

In the Americas there were many regional variations of Spanish advance and local resistance. In the south of what is now Chile, the

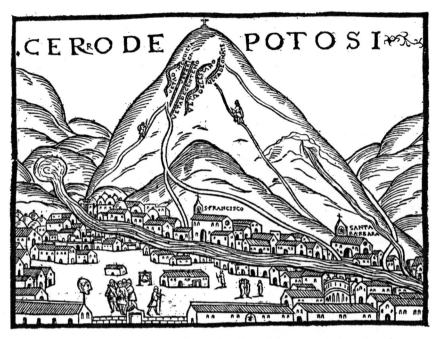

Men make their way up steep tracks on the silver-rich mountain looming above the churches and silver refineries of Potosí. The flow of silver from these highlands and later from Mexico linked Asia, Europe, Africa, and the Americas. Lilly Library, Indiana University, Bloomington.

Araucanian people defeated Spanish advances over and over again, and thus succeeded in remaining independent until the 1800s. On the northern frontier of the Spanish empire, the Pueblo peoples of what is now New Mexico rebelled and expelled the Spanish in 1680, but the conquerors came back early in the 1700s. In the core areas on which the whole structure rested, the Andes and highland Mexico, disruption, plunder, and disease had given way to a lesser sort of peace and accommodation. Native peoples had had elaborate customary hierarchies of rank, service, and distribution of goods that could not be put back together after the epidemics and the elimination of the supreme Aztec and Inca rulers. The Spaniards recognized local chiefs, who began to take on some of the way of life of a Spanish small landholder, including using the prefix "Don." Spanish settlers might get from the crown grants of land and rights to the labor of some Native American people. These grants were not technically inheritable, but formed along with the chiefs' holdings the foundations of the world of the Mexican estate, *hacienda*, often based in cattle ranching. In addition to the rents and services rural people owed to chiefs and landlords, the state made some claims on their labor, especially in the Andes, where the old Inca pattern of labor away from the home settlement was elaborated in a heavy burden of compulsory labor, called the *mita*, especially in the mines at Potosí in present-day Bolivia. In the cities, in the mines of Mexico, and increasingly in the Andes, Native Americans moved away from their home villages and worked for wages.

From the beginning Native American people had converted to Catholicism as they saw evidence of the superior power of the Christian God, but that did not mean that they gave up their old gods. Sometimes they took a Christian saint to be the same as an old god, and they performed prayers and ceremonies to both at once. The missionary priests struggled against these tendencies, but in fact they gave depth and color to Spanish American Catholicism; they are very much alive today. The Virgin Mary had a special appeal to people who had already worshipped mother goddesses.

From their beginnings, there was a great deal of ethnic mixing in the Spanish colonies, as Native American women bore the children of Spanish men. The rulers created elaborate classifications and names for different racial mixes. African slaves formed the largest part of the population in the islands, the coast of what now is Colombia, and in the bigger cities. Native American languages did not die—some of them are spoken today—but people of many backgrounds spoke to each other in Spanish. The town council, an institution brought from Europe and exploited by Cortés from the start, became a stronghold of local continuity and identity.

In the late 1600s we get a glimpse of the riches and ambiguities of this mixed or "creole" culture in the life of one of the greatest poets in the Spanish language, Sor Juana Inés de la Cruz. Born on the edge of Spanish-speaking society near the great Valley of Mexico, bookish and clever, she might have made an upward marriage into the colonial elite, but would have become completely subjected to her husband's will and needs. By becoming a cloistered nun she managed to keep most of her time for her wide and adventurous reading and writing, and for intelligent conversation with many visitors to her convent. Re-telling a classical Greek tale of the god Neptune changing a floating island into a stable one, she compared it to Tenochtitlán, originally built on "isles of floating grasses, by blind and ignorant heathen."[3] Always suspect in the eyes of conventional church authorities, in 1694 she finally was forced to surrender her library and scientific instruments and give up writing. During an epidemic in 1695 she devotedly cared for sister nuns, caught the disease, and died.

While the Spanish were conquering major pieces of North and South America, the Portuguese were sailing around Africa and across the Indian Ocean, and getting their own foothold in South America. Columbus had tried to pitch his project for a westward voyage to the spice-producing Indies to the king of Portugal before he turned to Spain. The Portuguese were very much interested in using nautical routes to reach the riches of Asia, but thought the better one was around the Cape of Good Hope. Portugal shared much of Spain's experience of Muslim rule and Christian Reconquista, but it had finished its shift to Christian political domination much earlier, in 1249. Between 1450 and 1700, this little corner of Europe sent ships and people out to an amazing variety of places. Portuguese missionaries converted a Congo king, who sent letters and envoys to his royal brother in Lisbon. Portuguese was spoken in ports on the coasts of India and modern Sri Lanka, Malaysia, and Indonesia and even on the south coast of China. A vast realm on the east coast of South America became a great center of sugar production and by 1700 was on the verge of supporting the Portuguese monarchy with vast resources of gold and diamonds; Brazilians still speak Portuguese today.

Geography had a lot to do with the dramatic outward turn of Portugal. Its fishermen sailed far out into the Atlantic in search of the codfish that have remained a staple of Portuguese cooking, and by 1500 were fishing on the Grand Banks off Newfoundland. Crusaders passing through the Strait of Gibraltar to attack the Muslims of the eastern Mediterranean sometimes stopped off to join in Portuguese attacks on the last Muslim strongholds in the south of the country, and some had settled and intermarried with the local elite. Italian merchants brought to Lisbon the products and attitudes of their trade with Muslim peoples around the Mediterranean—African gold and ivory and a few African slaves. By 1450 Italians, especially from the great port of Genoa, and merchants from all around the Iberian Peninsula, Catalans, Castilians, and Portuguese, had started to settle and fight over the Canary and Madeira islands off the coast of Africa, and the Portuguese had sailed straight out into the Atlantic to establish their first footholds on the previously uninhabited Azores. For Portugal, under a new line of kings after 1385, all this was closely tied to the defense of its independence from the rest of the peninsula, especially Castile.

The king's sons won their first great honors as knights in the conquest of Ceuta on the coast of Morocco in 1415, which helped to protect Italian merchants sailing in and out of the Mediterranean from Muslim pirates, and provided a base for Christian pirates and for direct access to the trade coming across the Sahara. But the impulse to fight

Muslims everywhere was very close to the surface; a Portuguese effort to take the port of Tangier in 1437 was a disastrous failure, and Portugal was stuck in intermittent nasty fighting in Morocco at least until 1577, when King Sebastian died in battle there. This led to a political crisis and sixty years (1580–1640) of Spanish domination of Portugal.

From about 1441 to his death in 1460, the leading promoter of Portuguese exploration down the African coast was Prince Henry, one of the princes knighted after the conquest of Ceuta in 1415. He has been called "the navigator," although he never sailed farther south on the African coast than Tangier, and a good deal of myth has built up about the purity of his scientific interest in exploration. He was a figure of his place and time, glorying in the capture and slaying of Muslims, always on the lookout for trading profits to support the next voyage.

His men established a trading post on Arguin Island, roughly at the north end of the coast of modern Mauritania, about 1440. In 1444 Prince Henry himself came to the southern Portuguese port of Lagos to see more than two hundred slaves bought or taken in raids along the African coast. Some of them were very dark sub-Saharan Africans, others paler people from the deserts and the islands. "When they watched the prisoners bound with rope being marched through the streets, the tumult of the people was so great as they praised the great virtues of the Prince.... As for the rest of [the slaves], the captains arranged for them to be auctioned in the city as a result of which each one secured great profit."[4] When Henry's men reached the mouth of the Senegal River around 1448, they sometimes managed to deal on friendly terms with the powerful kings of the Wolof people a few miles upstream and found that they had to stop taking slaves in violent raids because they now were facing more numerous and better-armed warriors who did not hesitate to attack the Portuguese ships in their big dugout canoes. The Portuguese knew the old caravan trade across the Sahara to the Mediterranean had brought gold from somewhere south of the Sahara, but they still could not find much. The Sahara trade also brought small numbers of slaves, often obtained in trade for horses that did not thrive in tropical Africa. Here the Portuguese had better luck, bringing horses to ports around the Senegal and Gambia rivers and taking back to Portugal several hundred slaves per year. In the 1460s and 1470s the Portuguese pushed farther down the west coast of Africa and fought a little war, the first European colonial war outside Europe, against Spaniards trying to get a share of the trade.

New possibilities opened up as the coast explored turned toward the east. Might they be on their way to the opening into the Indian

Ocean? There were legends of a Christian king somewhere to the east, called Prester John, who might be a valuable ally against Islam. In parts of what is now Nigeria the Portuguese visited rulers who had substantial walled towns and artisans producing magnificent bronzes, but they were not Prester John. A Portuguese envoy sent off south from Cairo did make contact with the Christian rulers of Ethiopia, but nothing came of the connection for many years. A more lasting success came with the founding, in 1481–82, of a permanent Portuguese trading castle on the coast of what is now Ghana, where it still can be seen. It is called Elmina Castle, from the Portuguese São Jorge del Mina, St. George of the Mine. The "mine" was the gold fields of the Ashanti country to the north, from which substantial amounts of gold were brought to the new trade center.

As the explorations continued, the coast of Africa turned south again, and the Portuguese opened a surprising connection with the kings of the Congo.[5] Several Congolese who had been taken to Lisbon returned in 1487 as Portuguese-speaking Christian converts. The Portuguese court sent missionaries, and a contender for the royal succession converted to Catholicism. He may have had some Portuguese help in defeating his rivals and emerging as king about 1506. He and others who became Christian seem to have sensed that the Portuguese had some previously unknown sources of power, which they saw when a missionary destroyed a traditional religious shrine, when Portuguese masons built solid stone houses, and not least when the soldiers fired their guns. Over the forty-year reign of Dom Affonso, the Christian king of the Congo, he exchanged many letters with the kings of Portugal, and the pope appointed one of Affonso's sons, educated in Europe, bishop of the Congo. The Portuguese royal court seems to have taken this relation very seriously and sent advisers, masons and other craftsmen, and more missionaries.

But even before Dom Affonso died in 1545 some grim realities were undercutting this dream of unforced conversion and cultural transformation. The island of São Tomé, north of the mouth of the Congo River, became an early center of Portuguese sugar cultivation, and large numbers of slaves were used. Portuguese residents in the Congo began trading in slaves, although the king was supposed to have complete control of the trade. Especially after Affonso's death, São Tomé people took sides in civil wars in the Congo. Slave trading and raiding spread inland and undermined the unity of the kingdom; it fell apart completely in the 1660s after a war with the Portuguese caused by their interference in Congolese civil wars.

Between 1487 and 1498 the world opened up for the Portuguese and the Spanish, and they acted as if it was all theirs. Ships commanded by Bartolomeu Dias reached the southern capes of Africa in 1481 and saw the open ocean stretching away to the east. Columbus made it across the Atlantic, and if he was not too clear about where he had been, it was clear that he had found something important. The pope proclaimed a dividing line running north and south around the Earth, dividing it between Spanish and Portuguese hemispheres, and the two monarchies signed a treaty shifting it a bit farther west so that the Portuguese would have the Azores. Then in 1497 Vasco da Gama set out with four ships and rounded Africa. Now the Portuguese were in a new world, a well-organized and prosperous Muslim maritime world. From modern Mozambique to modern Kenya, they found a series of splendid white cities where a Swahili-speaking African Muslim culture thrived and where Muslim traders had been coming and going regularly for hundreds of years. They managed to get good advice about following the monsoon winds across to India. They went ashore at Kozhikode (formerly spelled Calicut), capital of a small Hindu state, that had a large community of Muslim merchants from all around the Indian Ocean. The Muslims were amazed and alarmed by the arrival of "ferengi," or "Franks," as the Muslims called the people who had come to the eastern Mediterranean as Crusader aggressors. "What the Devil brought you here?" said one to Da Gama's men. "We came to seek Christians and spices."[6] The world around Da Gama's men was so strange to them that they seem to have thought the first Hindu temples they entered were Christian; Muslims did not worship images, so they took anyone who had images in a place of worship to be the only kind of non-Muslim they knew, a Christian: "And many, many other saints were painted on the walls of the church, with diadems, and their painting was different [from ours] because the teeth were so big they came out of the mouth a whole inch, and each saint had four or five arms."[7] The local Muslim traders were predictably hostile, and the presents the Portuguese brought were obviously ridiculous amid the jeweled splendor of the local ruler's court. A few swords were drawn, a few shots fired, but they got away without disaster.

As soon as Vasco da Gama reported back to Lisbon, the Portuguese knew they were onto something big, and every year they sent more ships. In 1500 relations at Kozhikode turned to open warfare, with shipboard cannon fired into the town, and the Portuguese found much more hospitality from a rival local ruler at Cochin a few miles down the coast, where they were allowed to build a fortified trading post. Everywhere around the Indian Ocean, rivalries among local rulers facilitated their making an alliance with one against the other. By about 1505 beginnings were made on a grand strategy to disrupt Muslim traders' commerce in spices and other goods from India to the Red Sea and the Persian Gulf. The Muslim powers did their best to retaliate, but they had to start from desert coasts where timber and food were scarce. In 1507–08 a fleet from Egypt defeated a Portuguese squadron but then was wiped out at Diu northwest of modern Mumbai. The Swahili towns of the east African coast were bullied into accepting Portuguese domination. Some Portuguese went on wild adventures inland, where gold mines had been reported, and later others intermarried and put down roots along the Zambesi River, so that Mozambique was a Portuguese colony until the late 1900s.

The Portuguese attacked the choke points on the Persian Gulf and Red Sea trade routes with mixed results. They took the island of Socotra off Yemen but found it to be uninhabitable because of lack of water. An attack on Aden in Yemen failed. They took and held Hurmuz at the mouth of the Persian Gulf. From 1509 to 1515 they laid more solid foundations and expanded to the east under the brilliant and ruthless governor Afonso de Albuquerque. On the west coast of India he took advantage of disunity and weakness among the Muslim kingdoms to conquer the coastal territory of Goa, which remained the center of Portuguese power in India until the 1900s. Aiming to control the trade in spices at the producing areas in eastern Indonesia or at a narrow strait between there and India, he sent an expedition that conquered and held the Muslim sultanate of Melaka in 1511. He sent others that established outposts in the Spice Islands but never fully dominated them and accomplished little except to kill, steal, and make enemies.

Beginning in 1518 the Portuguese got substantial footholds on the island we now call Sri Lanka (previously Ceylon) and continued to build up their presence on the west coast of India, from Diu to Goa to Cochin. After the conquest of Goa, Albuquerque had encouraged his men to marry widows of fallen members of the Muslim garrison; we might wonder what the ladies thought about being treated as part of the conquerors' loot. Albuquerque's action often is seen as a sign of a relatively relaxed Portuguese attitude to racial mixing, and the result all along this coast and in Sri Lanka was the emergence of a substantial "Indo-Portuguese" population, mixed in racial heritage and Catholic in religion, uniquely blending heritages of culture and custom. People with names like Souza and Da Silva are still found in these areas. The active support of these communities, including their participation in such European organizations as guilds, religious confraternities, and town councils, was a key to the persistence of Portuguese power and influence in the region, including successful resistance to Muslim counterattacks.

The Ottoman Empire sent a big fleet to India in 1535 and besieged Diu, which barely survived. But there was no sustained Muslim counterattack, and from the coasts of India, where timber and food would have been much more readily available than along the desert coasts to the north, there was no anti-Portuguese action except some small-scale piracy. The Portuguese claimed the right to control all sea trade leaving India and confiscated the cargo of any ship that did not have a Portuguese sailing permit, which would not be granted to the Muslim enemy. Portuguese attacks on ports and ships disrupted trade to the Red Sea and the Persian Gulf, but the systematic shutdown through the sailing permit system could not be sustained; a Muslim merchant could bribe Portuguese commanders to sell a permit, or a captain could be paid to let a ship go free when it had no permit. Once the Mughal rulers were in control of part of the coast, good relations with them seemed to require granting them a few permits, especially for ships carrying pilgrims to Mecca. Venetian records on trade in the eastern Mediterranean suggest that the flow of Asian goods was returning to normal after about 1550.

A Portuguese embassy had reached China as early as 1517, but it had accomplished nothing. In the 1540s Portuguese traders reached Japan for the first time, and in 1557 arrangements with local officials led to the establishment of a trading outpost at Macau, near modern Hong Kong. The Japanese imported large quantities of Chinese silks, whose quality they could not yet match, and paid for them largely with the growing output of gold, silver, and copper from their own mines. Japanese piracy had long been a menace on China's coast, so Japanese ships were not welcome there; the Portuguese got a big share of the profits of this trade.

The arrival of the Dutch East India Company in the Indian Ocean after 1600 reduced the Portuguese presence to a few tiny outposts, which they held until the 1900s: Goa and nearby places, Macau, and East Timor. They were gone from the Spice Islands by 1620; the Dutch took Melaka in 1641; and the posts on Sri Lanka and on the southwest coast of India had fallen by 1664.

The Portuguese ships sailing from Lisbon to Goa and beyond provided the shipping, the port bases, and some financial support for some of the most surprising cultural encounters of the early modern world, the Jesuit missions to the civilizations of Asia. The Jesuits traveled with the approval

Jesuits and other Roman Catholic missionaries presented the basics of the Christian gospel in Chinese, and they had Chinese printers copy images from European books. This woodblock print shows the temptation of Jesus in the wilderness. Bibliothèque Nationale, Paris, Chinois 6750.

of the kings of Portugal and to some degree under their control, but not all were Portuguese; many were Italian, and members of the China mission included Germans, Poles, and natives of what is now Belgium. They all brought to their encounters with Asia characteristics of the Society of Jesus since its founding by Ignatius of Loyola and his companions in the 1530s: efforts to influence the lives and beliefs of the upper classes by direct contact and by the education of their sons; a special sympathy for the bravery and loyalty of the aristocratic soldier; and a conviction that science and scholarship, especially the study of the ancient Greeks and Romans, could support and refine Christian belief and education.

One of the most dramatic of these Jesuit encounters occurred in Japan, where regional lords in search of the profits of trade sometimes befriended the missionaries who came with the merchants. The Jesuits found in the samurai codes of honor and elegance of social convention at least equal to their own; they often felt like children as they learned how to make themselves socially acceptable. They encountered a society in which the old moral codes were not working very well, and some people of all classes were ready to make a radical commitment to something new. The desire to bring Portuguese trade profits to their ports also motivated some of the daimyo (regional lords) and samurai to become Christian. Some of the artisans, merchants, and farmers came to Christianity as others came to radical Buddhist sects that bound commoners together in rejection of samurai authority. Several hundred thousand Japanese became Catholic. To their rulers they began to look like two kinds of political threat: regional under Christian daimyo and local against all samurai authority.

The Jesuits learned the difficult language, set up a printing press, adapted Christian art to Japanese tastes, and opened a seminary to educate future Japanese priests. They learned to explain how their religion was not just another form of Buddhism, and to use some of the moral rhetoric of Chinese traditions long influential in Japan, but they did not have to adjust their teaching to the resistance of a single dominant local belief system, simply because there was no one such system at this time. Beginning in 1592, the authorities who were creating new kinds of political order took measures against missionaries and converts as threats to that order. From 1612 on, persecution was brutally thorough. Many missionaries and thousands of Japanese died for their faith, sometimes under terrible torture. By 1640 there were only tiny remnants of Japanese Catholicism deeply hidden, and the Portuguese had been expelled from Japan. The martyrs proved that Catholic teaching had fallen on fertile soil in Japan and that the Jesuits had known what they were doing.

Some of the Jesuits making basic policy for the Japan effort were based in Macau, and their experiences in Japan influenced their approach to China, where limits on contact with foreigners and a long-established Confucian orthodoxy presented a different set of challenges. The traditional scholar-official elite was firmly in control of the government and confident of its own basic values; yet to many thoughtful Chinese around 1600, it seemed that lavish spending and governmental corruption were violating the conscientious scholarship and public service at the center of the Confucian tradition. The selfless commitment that had prompted the Jesuits to voyage so far from home impressed these Chinese, as did the solidity and usefulness of their knowledge of astronomy, geography, and much more. The Jesuits, especially the brilliant Italian Matteo Ricci, came to respect the scholars' moral quest, and to argue that Christian teachings in fact supported and supplemented Confucian teachings and helped to combat a tendency to irresponsibility that had come from Buddhism. They spent a great deal of time studying the Chinese language, and aroused some interest among Chinese scholars in their maps of the world and their astronomical skills. As they studied the classical Chinese texts, the Jesuits even began to argue that the ancient sages had known of the true God, only to lose that knowledge later as a result of Buddhist influence. In all this the Jesuits were pupils of some remarkable scholar-officials, several of whom became Christian converts. When Xu Guangqi, a major scholar, became a high official in the late 1620s, he opened the way for the Jesuits to demonstrate their skills in observational astronomy at the imperial court, where the calibration of the annual calendar was an important function of government. The Jesuits' methods were found more accurate than those then in use, and from the 1630s until after 1700, Jesuits were employed at the Imperial Board of Astronomy. Their position at court provided political cover for missionaries and converts in the provinces, even though Christianity was not formally granted toleration until 1692.

Scholar-officials like Xu Guangqi would not have converted to a religion that did not allow them to pay traditional homage to their ancestors. Aspiring scholars had to attend annual ceremonies honoring the great sage Confucius. The Jesuits were convinced that a modified form of the ancestral ceremonies, and attendance at the Confucian ceremonies, were not parts of a non-Christian religion and could thus be permitted to their converts. The Chinese Christians would join Christ and Confucius in a way similar to the Jesuits' own joining of Christ with the noble heritage of Greek and Roman moral philosophy. There were many shades of opinion among the missionaries and some outright rejection of the Jesuit accommodations. The Jesuits continued to study and to write about China; in 1687 a magnificent translation of some key Confucian texts was published in France, a monument in the growing interchange among the great cultures of the early modern world.

A third remarkable example of the Jesuits' encounter with Asian cultures was the work of Roberto de Nobili in south India from 1612 to 1656. Nobili was very much impressed by some of the learned and highly spiritual teachers in the branch of Hinduism focused on the worship of the god Vishnu. Quite a few Catholic and Protestant clergymen residing in India in the 1500s and 1600s came to respect the austerity and single-mindedness of Hindu holy men even when they thought the content of their beliefs nonsensical. Nobili learned the very difficult Tamil language, and composed in Tamil introductions to Christian belief and long song-poems with Christian themes. He and his close followers began to dress in an adaptation of the dress of Hindu holy men. Many other Catholics in India were horrified, and the controversy eventually was referred all the way to Rome. Nobili does not seem to have made much of a breakthrough toward a self-sustaining Catholic community in India, but his response to an apparently alien way of spiritual life remains an impressive piece of early modern interconnection.

Conditions for missionary work seemed more favorable in the Mughal Empire in northern India, where the great Muslim emperor Akbar liked to listen to disputes among teachers of various religions, and was especially inclined to give a respectful hearing to Christianity because Mary the mother of Jesus is revered in Islam. Artists and craftsmen working for the Jesuits produced some wonderful religious paintings drawing on both Indian and European traditions, and spectacles like one Nativity scene at court: "an ape which squirted water from its eyes and mouth, and above it a bird which sang mysteriously...and a globe of the world supported on the backs of two elephants...Around the Holy Infant in the crib were some sayings of the Prophets who pretold the coming of God into the World."[8] But the Jesuits did not win many converts, and later in the 1600s the Mughals turned toward a narrower Islam.

Around the south Atlantic, cultural encounter and missionary work developed in the very different contexts of frontier societies with plantation agriculture and slave labor. The placement of the latitude line dividing the Spanish and Portuguese spheres in the Atlantic turned out, as more of the coast of South America was mapped, to have left a large piece of that continent, the eastward bulge of modern Brazil, on the Portuguese side of the line. For several decades the Portuguese did not settle much. They bought from the Native American peoples some large tree trunks that produced an excellent red dye. The wood came to be called brazil wood because its color reminded people of red-hot coals, or *brazos* in Portuguese. Portuguese ships returning from the Indies swung far out into the south Atlantic and occasionally stopped on the Brazil coast; the Portuguese kept a few ships and soldiers there to protect the ships coming from the Indian Ocean from French pirates. From the 1540s on there was a more substantial effort to build up a colonial government, partly in response to the rapid development of sugar cane cultivation, brought from islands off the coast of Africa. The harvesting and processing of sugar cane required nonstop labor in brutal heat, and on the African islands this already was being done with enslaved African labor. The Portuguese enslaved large numbers of Brazilian Native Americans, but new diseases reduced their already sparse populations. Soon African slaves were brought to Brazil. By the 1620s almost all the slaves on the plantations were from Africa. Another important cash crop was tobacco, some of which was sold in the trade in West Africa, along with the rum that was a byproduct of sugar-making. Slaves became expert managers of the sugar refining process and skillful carpenters, smiths, and horsemen.

Work on a sugar plantation at harvest time was brutal. Discipline was enforced with the whip, imprisonment, hot lard or hot wax on the skin, or cutting off ears and noses; some slaves were driven to suicide. But still the slaves managed to keep some of their African music and religion alive; they are important parts of Brazilian culture today. A large population of mixed racial heritage grew up, the product of relations (frequently coerced) between white men and female slaves. Some slaves managed to escape to form big autonomous settlements in the back country, one of which survived Portuguese attacks for almost a hundred years.

Dutch attacks on the Portuguese holdings around the south Atlantic began in the 1620s. They took Elmina on the modern coast of Ghana in 1637 and the ports of modern Angola in 1641. By the 1630s, they came to hold much of the prosperous sugar-growing territory along the northeast coast of modern Brazil. From 1637 to 1644 this Dutch conquest zone had as its governor Joan Maurits van Nassau Siegen, a relative of the semi-hereditary military commanders of the Dutch Republic. He was one of the more astute colonial rulers of early modern times, taking a great interest in gathering information about the area, consulting with leading Portuguese who stayed to try to make the best of the situation, even convening an informal assembly. But after he was recalled, a guerrilla war waged by Portuguese sympathizers, many of them partly Native American or African in culture and heritage, pushed the Dutch back and out by 1654.

Sugar was a coastal crop for reasons of climate and transportation. Until about 1620 the Portuguese had not touched most of the vast inland areas of modern Brazil. In the 1620s and 1630s there were several big expeditions into the vast jungles and encounters with many Native American peoples of the Amazon basin, but still little sustained connection. The real thrust inland came from far to the south, in the region around modern São Paulo. The troops of adventurers who set out on long expeditions were called *bandeirantes*, from the flags, *bandeiras*, under which they rode. Most of them were of mixed Portuguese and Native American parentage, and they usually spoke a Native American language, not Portuguese. Their multi-cultural origins, their boldness in opening up the interior, and their key role late in the 1600s in discovering the great sources of gold and diamonds that transformed Brazil after 1700 have made the bandeirantes figures of immense glamour and importance to modern Brazilians, who usually manage to forget that in their early years the main business of the bandeirantes was taking Native American slaves.

The bandeirantes and the plantation owners whom they supplied with slaves had been opposed since the late 1500s by Jesuit missionaries, who learned native languages and worked hard to re-settle Native Americans in big settlements where they could be protected from the bandeirantes and taught to be better Christians. The most influential of these Jesuits, Antonio Vieira, claimed to find in the Old Testament prophecies of a Christian empire in the Amazon that would open the way to the universal victory of Christianity, if only the missionaries would learn Native American languages and be allowed to protect their converts from the bandeirantes. His vision is still part of the moral heritage of multiracial Brazil today.

The Spanish-Portuguese division of the world, and vagueness about just where the line actually was, had another singular consequence halfway around the world from the Atlantic line. Spanish voyages across the Pacific became the longest regular maritime voyages of the early modern world, making a powerful set of economic connections among miners in the Andes, indigenous peoples and European settlers in a corner of maritime Southeast Asia, and merchants, craftsmen, and peasants in the booming economy of China. It all started with the first voyage around the world, commanded by Ferdinand Magellan, a Portuguese seaman serving the Spanish crown. Magellan's ships found their way through the formidable straits that now bear his name at the southern tip of South America, and made the immense voyage out of sight of land across the south Pacific. Magellan was killed in a fight with indigenous people on Cebu Island in the modern Philippines in 1521; his commanders eventually brought the survivors home to Spain. As Spanish power reached across the Isthmus of Panama and down the west coast of South America, there were several more voyages of exploration across the Pacific.

In the islands that the Spanish would name Philippine after their King Philip II, the trade-driven expansion of Islam had reached the southern islands, especially Mindanao and Sulu, but not the northern ones. As Spanish probes became more regular in the 1560s, they found Chinese traders around Cebu and Iloilo. At the magnificent harbor of Manila Bay, they found a local ruler and a few Chinese. In 1571 they attacked the local ruler and established their own authority. The following year the new settlement barely survived an attack by Chinese pirates. Although Spanish-Chinese hostility would recur many times, the two sides soon realized that each represented an enormous opportunity for the other if they could get along.

China in the late 1500s was in a phase of energetic growth of trade and production of its fine craft goods, including silks, porcelain, and lacquerware. Until 1350 or 1400 it had had a sophisticated system of paper money used in large transactions and long-distance trade, but that had collapsed as a result of bad management. Now large-scale transactions were paid for in silver, but supplies were less and less adequate as trade grew, so that anyone who could pay for Chinese goods in silver earned an extra profit on the currency transaction. The silver from the mines of Potosí, the Andes, and later Mexico was supposed to pay for goods from Spain and serve as tax revenue to support Spain's armies in Europe. However, the profits of using it to buy Chinese goods were very attractive, and the silks and porcelain soon became features of the lavish consumption of the viceroys' courts in Mexico City and Lima. It was said that in Lima's great households the African slaves were dressed in Chinese silks.

From the 1580s to 1815, a "Manila Galleon" or two loaded with silver sailed every year for Manila from Acapulco on the west coast of Mexico. With good tropical winds the westbound voyage was pretty much a straight line. The return to Acapulco required a long detour to the north to pick up prevailing winds, missing the Hawaiian Islands and occasionally sighting the coast of what are now California and Baja California. These were the longest regular voyages out of sight of land of early modern times. Manila was an indispensable but largely passive connection point, where the Chinese merchants brought their goods and took away silver. Little was done to develop even the rich agricultural areas near Manila until long after 1700. A resident Chinese community far outnumbered the Spaniards and dominated all the trades. A few Chinese converted to Catholicism, and from about 1600 on the Spanish always appointed one of the converts as "Captain" over his countrymen. Constant tension over tax collection and trade issues led to big outbreaks of violence and massacres of the Chinese in 1603 and 1639, but the Chinese and the Spanish always remembered pretty quickly that they needed each other.

In the official Spanish view the Philippines were a Catholic realm, and the expense of maintaining the colony was largely justified by its work in converting the heathen. Contacts with the Muslim peoples of Mindanao and Sulu always were hostile. The great missionary orders-Jesuit, Franciscan, Dominican, and Augustinian-sent many priests. Their big estates were a very important part of the Spanish presence outside of Manila and on other islands. The Filipinos sometimes exasperated the fathers with their jokes and guessing games, but in the long run they found things in Catholicism that made sense in terms of their own cultural inheritance—godparents, holy water, spectacle and ceremony—and became Asia's only Roman Catholic people. The University of Santo Tomas in Manila, still a major university today, was founded as a Dominican seminary in 1611, twenty-five years before Harvard was founded in North America. The Dominicans had special responsibility for efforts to convert the Chinese; they found some of them tenacious in their non-Christian beliefs and practices, but many of them asked good questions and some became zealous Catholics. Some of these Dominicans carried their efforts into China itself, establishing convert communities in one part of Fujian province that have survived every persecution and government control effort. The Manila galleons are a distant memory, but the improbable cultural connections they made possible live on.

Columbus and Vasco da Gama didn't suddenly turn a medieval world into an early modern one, but they were catalysts of big processes that linked the continents, brought silver, spices, and sugar to Europe, and opened up a world in which amid plunder and brutality Italian Jesuits and Chinese scholars could learn from each other.

CHAPTER 3

Old Ways Made New, 1530–1570

In the world of 1450 to 1700, many people were dissatisfied with the religious and moral life around them, but almost no one wanted to make a radical break with tradition. They dreamed of the old gods and the ancient sages. Europeans wanted a renaissance, that is, a rebirth of the noble ways of ancient Greece and Rome. They wanted not a break with Christianity, but a purification, a reformation. Asians sought a personal vision of the god Krishna or a pure way to become sages themselves, morally perfect people, like the ancient teacher Confucius and the sage kings he revered.

These proclamations were not just smoke screens to hide innovation from the guardians of orthodoxy or delusions on the parts of the innovators. Every tradition as it is handed down loses its freshness, becomes routine, makes its peace with practices against which it once struggled, and becomes in one way or another established and comfortable. Especially when the original passions and visions are preserved and passed down in writing, there always are people who carefully read the records of the original vision or revelation and cannot get over the gap between the original purity and the current routine. Back to the gospel message! The way of the sage kings can be found today! True Muslims must abandon all these pagan practices! But each great tradition is a tangled skein of continuities and interactions, not a monolith, and the would-be reviver sometimes re-braids them in strands of the old ways and new practices and interpretations in skeins whose novelty startles even their maker.

In Europe in the fifteenth and sixteenth centuries, new passions for the ancient world interacted in very confusing ways with re-shapings and revivals of Christianity. For example, any selection of great Renaissance paintings provides examples of Biblical scenes and of scenes from Greco-Roman mythology or history, rendered in the same glorious techniques and finishes. People all over Western Europe contributed to these changes, but they always looked to Italy for leadership and great examples; think, for example, of the Italian settings of many of Shakespeare's plays.

Since the 1300s Italian scholars had been calling for more study of the great ancient masters in Latin and more efforts to write Latin as they did, not the late medieval Latin that was the main language of formal written expression in recent centuries. The study of ancient Latin and the writing of letters and essays in ancient style soon led to careers that combined scholarship, politics, and literary fame.

In 1400 very few intellectuals in Western Europe could read Greek. The siege and fall of Constantinople increased interest, and refugee Greek scholars taught their language and literature, especially in Italy. About 1460 an Italian monk brought to Florence a Greek manuscript of a set of texts soon translated into Latin and known as the Hermetic Corpus. The Hermes of the texts was the Greek god of writing and messages, called Mercury in Latin. But these texts and the teachings that grew up around them gave them an even longer pedigree in human wisdom; Hermes was Thoth, the Egyptian god of writing, and perhaps also Moses.

The Hermetic texts taught "The world is always a living animal—nothing in the world is mortal. Since every single part...is always living and is in a world which is always one and always a living animal, there is no place in the world for death." Souls were reincarnated under the rule of different gods, depending on their special natures. Man himself was a god, formed by the creator god to contemplate and serve the created universe. All of this was thought compatible with Christianity, simply showing it to be a part of a more ancient wisdom; a picture of Hermes could be found in the cathedral in Siena.[1]

The Hermetic teachings were meant to be for a select few of the most intelligent and spiritual, not for the ordinary man. They made it possible for quite a few early modern intellectuals to be interested in all kinds of ideas about nature, even astrology (the calculation of individual destinies through the stars) and alchemy (the search for methods to turn ordinary metals into gold), while insisting that they were good Christians. Prospero in Shakespeare's *The Tempest*—yes, an Italian—is a Renaissance man, a magnificent English portrait of a type well-known in Shakespeare's London. Johannes Kepler and Tycho Brahe, basic contributors to the new astronomy, were deeply involved with astrology. Even Newton was interested in alchemy. The profusion of patterns of meaning Renaissance men were interested in, and their greater interest in the evidence of their senses, did more to open the way to science than some of these "pre-scientific" views did to lead them astray.

It can be very hard to really appreciate the zeal of scholars to preserve, study, and interpret their ancient texts, whether they are the Vedas, the Chinese classics, the dialogues of Plato, or the Bible. But Renaissance architecture provides an obvious path to understanding the passion for ancient Greece and Rome. In Florence, beside the modern mayhem of speeding motor scooters, rise the facades of the palaces its great families built in the 1400s, the stonework of their upper levels ornamented with meticulously regular arches in the Roman manner.

The Florentine identification with ancient Rome was rooted in idioms and institutions of city and citizenship that seemed to come straight from ancient Rome. Florence in the 1440s was intensely proud of its

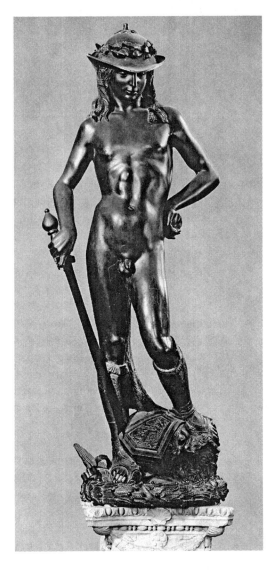

The Old Testament story of David's victory over Goliath is celebrated in Donatello's statue, and so is the beauty of the human body. The statue was commissioned by the Medici family, rulers of Florence. Erich Lessing / Art Resource, NY.

broadly participatory political structure, had survived attacks by more powerful city-states, and was at the zenith of its own power. David's victory over Goliath was a favorite Biblical story. The David theme was the first to carry Renaissance art into a startlingly un-medieval celebration of the human body, in a bronze statue of David by Donatello.

This statue, commissioned by the great Medici family in the 1440s, was the first free-standing male nude since antiquity. Another Medici commission, the painting "The Birth of Venus" by Sandro Botticelli, completed after 1482, gives some sense of the ways in which Greek myth could convey something of the same sense of a world alive and full of wonder. In his lovely nude Venus blown gently ashore on a seashell, Botticelli shows that at the highest level there is no incompatibility between the passions of the flesh and our highest spiritual aspirations.

Florence's city government, the church, guilds, and great families spent lavishly on beautiful churches, palaces, guild halls, and finely finished paintings and sculptures, most movingly in the many "annunciations," as the blessed Virgin raises her hand in mild surprise and simple acknowledgement of the angel's astounding news. Splendid renditions of international cityscapes and landscapes, costumes and human types, enliven nativities and other Biblical scenes. The Italy of the Renaissance was deeply involved with its eastern neighbors. Turbans, Byzantine church architecture, even a giraffe, enliven a painting of Saint Mark preaching in Alexandria by Giovanni and Gentile Bellini. The Bellinis worked for years at a time at the Ottoman court. Classical revival columns and arches, designed by Italian architects, graced facades in Istanbul.

These are not the only ways in which the splendors of the Renaissance were linked to a world of trade and of often brutal politics. Young men flocked to the academies to learn elegant Latin not just out of love of antiquity but also because good Latin might lead to a position as a secretary of a great man or in a municipal government. The mixes of career and ideal were not too distant from those that made classically educated young men the rulers of British India in the 1800s or make a Harvard or Yale degree a stepping stone to a New York bank or law firm in our own time.

In one remarkable Italian thinker, Niccoló Machiavelli, who wrote in the early 1500s, we even find something that looks very much like a beginning of social science thinking. His book *The Prince* is a lucid and brutally honest policy paper on the conditions of political success and failure in the Italy of his own time. Lying and betrayal, he says, may be necessary to political survival. But occasionally in *The Prince*, and constantly in his longer and perhaps richer *Discourses*, an amazing

In Botticelli's painting the winds gently blow the Greek goddess Venus toward shore. Renaissance Europeans' fascination with the ancient Greeks joins with celebration of the beauties of nature and humankind. Erich Lessing / Art Resource, NY.

depth of knowledge of ancient Greece and Rome informs his reasoning. Rome lives for him not as a noble ideal but as a real and brutal world very much like his own. Machiavelli's discussions of ancient Rome are recoveries of a remote past as uncanny and sophisticated as Botticelli's *Birth of Venus*.

Many who are moved by the Renaissance's delight in human beauty would like to think that these changes helped to liberate women from medieval patriarchy and misogyny. The evidence is scattered and mixed. Venice, rich and cosmopolitan, was known for its sophisticated "honest courtesans," who supported themselves by their sexual liaisons, both long- and short-term, but sometimes also were welcome participants in the most refined literary salons. But closer examination shows that Venetian wives and daughters were kept under unusually tight control, and the courtesans can be seen as welcome ornaments in an overwhelmingly male high society as well as alternative sexual outlets for young aristocrats who scarcely saw young women of their own class.

The impulse to revive and reshape a great heritage can look very different when that heritage is religious, passionate for a reality beyond the limitations of human power, knowledge, and mortality. In the early 1500s in rich and populous Bengal, today divided between Bangladesh and the Indian state of West Bengal, a great religious teacher called Sri Krishna Caitanya[2] brought to its fullest expression the long development of a kind of passionate devotion to the Hindu god Vishnu and especially to his manifestation in the form of the god Krishna. This devotion was expressed in ecstatic chanting and dancing, in which every Hindu could participate without reference to most of the traditional barriers of caste and sex.

In the Hindu tradition, a system of castes, groups that married within themselves and avoided many forms of contact with other groups, had evolved and elaborated for many centuries. The interpretation of sacred texts and the practice of the ceremonies they prescribed became the core duties of the brahmins, the top-ranked priestly group. People believed that accumulation of good or bad deeds determined the caste into which one was reborn, while those of deeper insight and compassion sought means to escape from the remorseless wheel of rebirth and to rescue others from it. Hinduism produced philosophical works of the most amazing elaboration and sophistication; an unparalleled richness of visualizations of the gods in temples that legitimized Hindu kingship; and great cycles of tales of the battles of gods, demons, and warrior aristocrats. Part of one of these cycles is the magnificent Bhagavad Gita, in which a warrior aristocrat is appalled by the possibility that he may kill relatives or old teachers in the next battle, but his charioteer teaches him the importance of selflessly fulfilling the duties of his place in society. The charioteer then reveals himself as the great god Krishna, and the Gita becomes one of the first texts that opens the possibility of simple and direct personal encounter with and devotion to that god as a religious practice as powerful as the elaborate ceremonies prescribed by the ancient Hindu texts or world-renunciation.

This focus on *bhakti*, devotion or encounter, first seems to have become a major part of Hinduism in the south of India in the 1000s and became a really major trend in the north after 1400. Bhakti texts are fervently emotional poems and songs of praise in one vernacular language or another, not in the classical Sanskrit. Thus they could be understood, and the emotions expressed in them shared, by ordinary people, not just by brahmins. The struggles of learned brahmins to assemble and edit texts and systematize their philosophical implications had little to offer ordinary people.

Furthermore, in the north, including Bengal, the rulers were Muslim. There were no Hindu rulers to spend lavishly on building temples or to support brahmins and Vedic ceremonies. The simple chanting and dancing of bhakti had great appeal in this situation. And no god was more accessible, more open to bhakti, than Krishna. For the bhakti devotee, constant repetition of the names of the gods—Hare Krishna Hare Krishna, Krishna Krishna Krishna Hare Hare (Hail Krishna, Hail Krishna, Krishna Krishna Krishna Hail Hail)—immediately brought one into the presence of the god. The true devotee might repeat the name of the god thousands of times a day. Anyone could participate; neither brahmin standing nor literacy, much less in Sanskrit, was required. But in the understanding of the bhakti devotee there was nothing new in these forms of devotion. Krishna was in the ancient texts, and so was the sense of the ease with which the divine and the human interconnected, especially by calling on the name of the god.

Krishna is considered an aspect of the great god Vishnu, and his worshippers often are called *Vaisnavas*, Vishnu worshippers. The core images of this personal devotion are passionate. Young women cannot resist the sight of the cowherd Krishna or the sound of his flute. Trembling with guilty desire, they flee their husbands to join him in trysts deep in the woods. Popular pictures of Krishna and his prime beloved, Radha, show them so thoroughly entwined that it is hard to see where one body ends and the other begins. Krishna is often represented with uncanny deep blue or emerald green skin, entwined with golden-bodied Radha.

Visvambhara, who later would adopt the religious name Krishna Caitanya (he who makes men aware of Krishna), was born in 1486 in a brahmin household in a Bengal village with a strong tradition of learning. Some stories are told of the uneasy situation of the brahmins under Muslim rule, but in his early years the clever young man and his parents were comfortable with his pursuit of a bookish Sanskrit education and the beginnings of a career as a schoolteacher. When he was twenty-two, he went to the great pilgrimage city of Gaya to perform funeral ceremonies for his father. Something happened; for the rest of his life he would simply dissolve in tears when he tried to explain it.

Back in his native village, he led his friends in evenings of dancing and singing the name of Krishna that soon spilled out of the courtyards into great processions through the streets. Established brahmins quite rightly saw a threat to their control of religious life, and pointed out to Muslim rulers the dangers to public order of uncontrollable mass meetings. But Caitanya reasoned calmly with an angry Muslim ruler who eventually himself became a devotee of Krishna. Hinduism had not previously been a missionary religion, and there was no clear way for an outsider to convert to it; these stories mark a major step toward a conception of Hinduism comparable to the religions of universal accessibility, Christianity, Islam, and Buddhism.

To spread his message and perhaps to let the tensions in his home town cool down a bit, Caitanya took the vows of a *sannayasin*, a wandering world-renouncer, traveling with a minimum of goods and comfort from temple to temple, holy site to holy site, far down into south India and then across to the great plains of the west and north. This was and is a venerated role in Hinduism, which some take up only after they have fulfilled the responsibilities of raising and providing for a family. All sannayasin are seekers and pilgrims; Caitanya also was a missionary for his new devotional practices and insights.

We have a great deal of pious legend and very little reliable information about this journey, which lasted from 1508 to 1510. Unable to speak the local languages, Caitanya still was able to exchange views with temple priests and with other sannayasin in Sanskrit. He had begun his journey at Puri, near the east coast southwest of Bengal, and settled there at its end. By that time, he was accompanied by devoted disciples who saw him not just as a great teacher but as the great god Krishna himself, taking on human form to bring a simple, accessible mode of worship to a decadent age. In a final twist that distinguished his teaching from other Vaisnava schools, his most devoted follower saw him manifest the golden body color of Krishna's consort, Radha; from then on, her anguished longing for Krishna took Caitanya over completely, and he was more and more out of touch with the ordinary human world.

All religions, of course, claim some kind of privileged access to realities beyond the ordinary human realm. "Read the Quran, God's Last Word." "Trust in Jesus, God's Only Son." "Awaken to the undivided Buddha Mind in which you already share." And so on. Almost all religions have some place for divine madness and for the holy fool, who sees things we don't see and doesn't cope very well with the things the rest of us see. The Bengali Vaisnavas insisted that the human and divine realities were parallel and interpenetrating. For some the celebration of the god in singing and dancing, the dazzling temple images, an occasional dream of Lord Krishna among the milkmaids, were enough. But Caitanya was not ordinary. He longed to spend all his time in the presence of his lord. When his disciples woke him from a beautiful dream of Krishna, he howled with remorse and longed to go back. He raced for the surf in pursuit of a vision of Krishna and was barely saved from drowning. For the last thirteen years of his life he was watched over constantly by his followers. The most intense longing was the only right state of mind for his non-visionary moments. His followers eventually

The god Krishna converses with a friend of his beloved Radha. Vivid images spread emotional devotion to Krishna among Hindus of all classes. Freer Gallery of Art, Smithsonian Institution, Washington, DC: Purchase F1991.2.

explained to themselves that the great god Krishna had wanted to incarnate in himself the most perfect form of religious devotion, and to do so, he had not just come to earth in Caitanya's person but had transformed that person into the passionately longing Radha.

These theological elaborations are less important than the universally accepted practices—singing, dancing, chanting the names of the gods—and the beautiful poetry they have inspired, all of which live on in Bengal to this day and in the twentieth century were spread around the world by the Krishna Consciousness Society, the "Hare Krishnas." Images of Krishna and of Caitanya's golden-skinned ecstasy are commonly found on websites today. There is little evidence that Caitanya offered Bengal's poor and despised anything but occasional release in evenings of ecstatic chanting and dancing. Some would say that is quite a lot, when it comes with such intense and simple emotion as in the following chant by Caitanya: "Let the earth of my body be mixed with the earth my beloved walks on. Let the fire of my body be the brightness of the mirror that reflects his face. Let the water of my body join the waters of the pool he bathes in. Let the breath of my body be air lapping his tired limbs."[3]

Another great religious teacher in the Indian world of around 1500 was much more engaged with society. Nanak, who became the first *guru*, great teacher, of the Sikh religion, grew up in northern India, much more directly in the path of invading Mughal armies. He was brought up a Hindu, of a much less bookish kind than Caitanya. Islam was all around him, as a source of religious insight as well as of conquest and repression. He was much more likely to be impressed by the spiritual equality of all Muslim believers than Hindus elsewhere. In 1496 he had a deep religious experience that led him to proclaim, "There is neither Hindu nor Muslim."

As he and his first disciples traveled around northern India, they ignored the restrictions on social mixing among caste groups, preferring to stay with low-caste friends even when they had elite supporters. Rules about sharing food with other groups are strict in the caste society, and Nanak challenged them directly, eating with everyone. He organized charitable kitchens that fed anyone who was hungry. The gathering of Sikh followers for a common meal has remained one of the central features of this teaching.

Although many Hindus, like Caitanya, believed they had to withdraw from ordinary life to devote themselves entirely to their passionate spiritual quest, the Sikhs from Nanak believed that the ordinary life of business and family was the best form of a religious life. Guru Nanak's songs and teachings are full of simple images drawn from the lives of ordinary people and the ceremonies that marked their stages. In the succession of great gurus that followed, many composed poems and songs in simple language, using both Hindu and Muslim vocabulary. Their teachings are full of sharp criticisms of the corrupt power of Muslim judges and the fakery of Hindu holy men.

Gobind Singh, the last in the succession of gurus in the late 1600s, taught his followers to "let divine wisdom be your guru and enlighten your soul" not in a forest retreat but in the busy life of a city. In his time, the Islamic orthodoxy of the Mughal Emperor Aurangzeb and a Hindu revival seemed to leave less and less room for people who were "neither Hindu nor Muslim," and Gobind Singh had to assure his followers that it was lawful to take up the sword. By 1690 the Sikhs were fighting full-scale battles against Mughal forces. They have remained some of India's finest warriors as well as some of the best businessmen. And they have a different kind of guru; at the end of his life, Gobind Singh took a compilation of the songs and teachings of the gurus compiled around 1600 and proclaimed that this book, the Granth, would be the teacher of the Sikh people from then on. And so it is today.

China's three great traditions—Confucianism, Buddhism, and Daoism—all have displayed over and over great capacities for reform and renewal. Pilgrimages and visions have their places in the native Daoist tradition and especially in Buddhism, which brought with it from its Indian origins staggering riches of imagery and of abstract thought. Readers who have had some introduction to the Confucian tradition might not expect to find much vision and quest in it. It can seem prosy, skeptical, careerist, conscientious in pursuit of virtuous government. But Wu Yubi, probably the greatest Confucian alive in 1450, was a visionary.

Wu had several dreams in which Confucius himself and King Wen of the Zhou Dynasty (from the first millennium BCE), came to visit him. Even Wu's wife dreamed that Confucius had stopped outside their door and sent a servant in to ask if Wu was at home. Moreover, Wu Yubi, unlike Confucius and most Confucians of any age, had no interest in pursuing a career as a government official. But both in his dreams and in his withdrawal Wu was a genuine Confucian. Confucius himself had dreamed of the Duke of Zhou (King Wen's brother and a great hero of lore about ancient China). Confucius' deep optimism about the potentialities of the human mind was inseparable from his conviction that ordinary human beings had produced a perfect social order in the days of King Wen and the Duke of Zhou. Confucius had hoped to find a ruler who would employ him, but had not been willing to serve corrupt or illegitimate power. In such bad times, to pursue with passion dreams of a past when moral uprightness and social harmony had been real on earth, and to teach students who might live to serve more virtuous rulers, was the best way to preserve one's integrity and not at all political. Thus both dreams and withdrawals from public life were parts of the image of Confucius himself.

The very conspicuously alien Mongol Yuan Dynasty had been driven from China in 1368 and a new Chinese Ming Dynasty proclaimed. There were many reasons for thinking that Confucian ideals now would be more fully realized than they had been in many centuries, perhaps ever. For centuries the cultural reformers of the school the Chinese call Daoxue (dao shweh), the School of the Way, and we call Neo-Confucianism had struggled to purge Chinese society of Buddhist influences. The Neo-Confucians sought to put into practice standards of family and community life they believed were derived from the Chinese classics that presented a picture of an ideal society in the days of King Wen and the Duke of Zhou. They exhorted rulers and high ministers to follow classical models of limited, unwarlike, selfless rule.

In the early Ming the Neo-Confucians seemed to have triumphed, with the establishment of elaborate new imperial ceremonies and institutions and above all in the mandating of their interpretations of the classics in examinations, which were the only route into service in the imperial bureaucracy. The founding emperor of the Ming was a shrewd, brutal warlord who knew he needed the Neo-Confucian scholars if he was going to consolidate peace over his vast empire, but he had no use for their pretensions to independence of moral judgment and action.

His son came to the throne by overthrowing the founding emperor's grandson in a civil war. The usurper emperor's dispatch of great fleets into the Indian Ocean was only one of his uses for major political responsibilities of palace eunuchs, castrated males, who Confucians insisted should be employed only within the palace, supervising the women of the court. Wu Yubi, with all his high Neo-Confucian ideals, first came to the capital in the year of the usurper's victory. It was mortally dangerous to put anything on paper criticizing the usurper, but hints can be found that Wu and a few friends concluded that no upright scholar could serve such an illegitimate ruler.

Neo-Confucians taught that through a life of intense study and self-cultivation, each of us can develop those beginnings of human goodness all of us have within us and become sages, individuals with morally perfect pitch, as Confucius and the Zhou founders had been. No one should settle for a more modest goal than sagehood. To pursue this goal through study and meditation, and to teach students who become disciples, building on your ideas and your quest for sagehood, was a very common phase of life for the scholar out of office. Wu Yubi went much further, making no attempt to pass examinations or take office. His teaching centered on the recovery of the undivided human mind, which Confucians believed to be the root of moral behavior. For Wu, focused moral seriousness as a key to that discovery, and most unusually, early rising and hard farm work for himself and his students was an aid to achieving that seriousness.

Most major Confucian intellectuals of the late 1400s did take office. But several did so only very briefly, including several disciples of Wu Yubi who maintained his focus on the mind and on seriousness. One of these disciples, Lou Liang, received late in his life a visit from a strange, intense young man, son of a very high-ranking official, who later took the name Wang Yangming. Lou explained to Wang that the "investigation of things," the study of texts and facts advocated by the Neo-Confucians, opened the way to sagehood. This brief encounter was like a spark falling on tinder. Young Wang began a restless quest, testing his powers of observation of nature as well as his knowledge of texts, realizing that there could be no end to the "investigation of things." He withdrew into meditation, found that he could not stop thinking about his parents and then realized that those thoughts were part of the structure of his mind. He passed the exams, held routine offices, and hated the routine. And then he got involved in a major political confrontation.

In 1505 a silly young emperor, very much in the hands of some especially corrupt and power-hungry palace eunuchs, came to the throne. Officials who protested the eunuch domination of the court were beaten in open court and sent into exile in remote frontier stations. Some were assassinated along the way, and others died of malaria. Wang's modest post did not require him to speak up, but his Confucian convictions did. He in turn was beaten and sent to run a postal station in the malarial southwest. In the face of danger he became capable and brave, helping with the farm work and wood chopping, singing to his retainers to keep up their spirits. Like many Chinese, he bought his own coffin to make sure that it was properly done, and in the evenings he meditated in front of it.

It was this experience with the brutal consequences of political action, followed by nights of literal confrontation with his own mortality, that produced Wang Yangming's key breakthroughs in understanding the terrifying puzzles of the Neo-Confucian heritage. If the road to sagehood led through study and disciplined self-cultivation, how could it ever end? How can we ever act in a way that fully realizes the moral goodness within us? He now saw that "the ten thousand things are all complete within me"; his mind already had within it the basic principles that would simply be reinforced by study. He also understood that "knowledge and action are one"; the mind already has within it the capacity to distinguish good and evil and respond appropriately to them, and we will respond appropriately, as we do when we smell a bad smell and move away from it, if we don't allow selfish considerations of career or personal safety to interfere.

The most powerful eunuch died in 1510, and although the silly emperor still was on the throne, Wang's political career began to revive. As he traveled around, he lectured to large assemblies of scholars on his new insights. Wang was very successful in restoring peace to areas troubled by bandits and rebels, and dealt decisively with the very dangerous rebellion of a prince of the imperial house. Then from 1521 to 1527 he was out of office. He kept busy with lecturing and writing, and died in 1529 on his way back from an expedition to suppress a tribal rebellion in the southwest. In his retirement years many students flocked to him, and he pushed farther some of the radical implications of his core insights. The basic substance of the mind, he taught, could be realized only through unremitting moral effort. There was not any good or evil in its basic structure, but only in the movements of the will as we recognize them and respond appropriately.

Wang's lectures, writings, and the published records of his conversations profoundly affected many listeners and readers. There is no such thing, he said, as learning that doesn't involve action. As we learn we have doubts and inquire about them; that's a kind of action. We should make good use of the natural inclinations of people, as when people teaching children take advantage of their desire to move and make noise by having them sing and practice ceremonial walking and bowing. "Like plants beginning to sprout, if they are allowed to grow freely, they will develop smoothly. If twisted and interfered with, they will wither and decline." Some students learned to see the deep goodness waiting to develop in all people. Wang asked a student, "What did you see in your walk?" The student replied, "I saw that the people filling the street were all sages."[4]

Some followers of Wang Yangming took the teaching that there was no good or evil in the basic structure of our minds to permit any kind of anti-social or non-conformist behavior that came to their minds. Others responded to his insistence that knowledge and action were one by becoming more committed to political engagement and dealing with practical problems. Both trends were conspicuous in a China that was in moral and political crisis after 1600, beset by corruption and grid-lock at court, and riddled with scholars seduced by the high life of its great commercial cities.

One interesting response that seems to have subsided by 1600 was the preaching of Wang's moral message to large urban audiences, including many non-scholars. A key figure in that movement, Wang Gen, was the poorly educated son of a merchant family. Visiting the great shrines to Confucius at Qufu, Wang realized that Confucius had been just a man and that sagehood like his was open to each of us. About 1504, he had a dream in which the heavens were tearing apart and falling; he rose up to put them back in their place, and the common people greeted him with ecstatic gratitude. He decided that if he was going to be like the ancient sages, he would have to wear the same clothing they did. He called on the great Wang Yangming himself in his peculiar clothes, made his points stubbornly, and finally declared himself a disciple. His teachings were close to Wang's on many points, but placed more emphasis on the bodily wellbeing of ordinary people. These teachings appealed very strongly to many common people, some of whom devoted the rest of their lives to spreading them, summoning village people to mass meetings after harvest with moralizing lectures and group singing. This popularized Confucianism seems to have reached a peak around the middle of the 1500s and seems to have declined in the disruptions after 1600.

Martin Luther and Wang Yangming were contemporaries, both seeking to purify and revive a great teaching. They cannot have known of each other, and it is hard to imagine what they might have found they had in common. Wang's teaching was rooted in optimism about what human nature could be in this world. Luther's Christianity was centered on sinfulness of human nature and the need for God's salvation. The complex European movement we call the Protestant Reformation did much to set off processes of change reaching far beyond the religious sphere. Religious differences and differences of language and culture reinforced each other in Europe's multi-centered state system. Religious war and ghastly repression, with many people burned at the stake for their beliefs, fuelled cycles of war and violence and eventually led some very wise people to principles of religious toleration. Religious and cultural changes clearly had some connection to the emergence of semi-democratic forms of politics and perhaps to the new values and practices of some great commercial cities. At the core of this great upheaval and change was a call for return to the lost fundamentals of Christianity.

The preacher's exhortation to turn away from the vanities of this world and to accept the salvation offered by Jesus Christ is at the heart of Christianity. It shaped a confusing and sometimes contradictory variety of movements of reform and revival in the 1400s. For some, an urban, commercial society with its free spending, fancy clothes, and sexual license provoked outrage and calls for repentance. Political thinkers and many churchmen saw corruption in the Roman Catholic Church as the core of the problem, but even among them there were many who hoped that a suitably reformed Catholic Church would be the solution.

In world-historical perspective, the Church of Rome was a most peculiar institution, having little territorial or military power but using a highly centralized bureaucracy and developed legal system to maintain unity of teaching and practice, and to influence believers. It proclaimed crusades against the Ottomans, divided the world between Spain and Portugal, grappled with the conundrums of missionary encounter with sophisticated non-Christian cultures, and contributed to political polarization in one country after another. At various times between 1000 and 1400, it had seemed possible that the Church of Rome would be securely subordinated to the Holy Roman Emperors, as the Greek Church was to the Byzantine, or that the Church would turn into a theocracy that could install or depose emperors, kings, and lesser lords. Neither project was entirely dead in the 1400s, but the reality was a set of messy and cynical compromises, in which kings obtained the right to name bishops in their own realms and agreed to the collection of church dues as long as they got a percentage. Europe's development of many political units in a variety of forms—hereditary monarchy, elective monarchy, aristocratic republic, and so on probably could not have sustained itself if the Roman Catholic Church and Holy Roman Empire had not checkmated each other. The Church's monopoly of access to the sacraments, the threat of excommunication and thus theoretically of dying without the possibility of salvation, were real enough, but if they were used too forcefully in pursuit of the worldly political goals of the papacy or in repression of powerful religious changes they could backfire, as they did in dealing with an obscure German monk named Martin Luther.

Luther's father had started out working in the copper mines and had risen to success in the smelting and foundry business. School and university offered a way into elite occupations for a talented young man from a well-off family of non-elite background. At university Luther already hated Aristotle and Aquinas, the great medieval authorities, but that hardly was unusual in his times. He was setting out to study the law when he was caught out in the open during a lightning storm and cried out that if he was saved he would become a monk. When he became a priest and celebrated his first mass, his father, appalled by this waste of a son of worldly promise, said of that lightning storm, "Take care that it was not an evil spirit."[5] His talents did not go unnoticed within the monastery walls; he gave brilliant lectures on the psalms and the New Testament.

In 1510 and 1511 Luther went to Rome on business for his order and was appalled by the immorality, cynicism, and luxury of the papal court. Then in 1517 he raised sharp questions about the sale of indulgences. Fifteenth-century Roman Catholics who feared eternal damnation for their sins (and who did not?) would confess their sins to a priest and would be told what kind of penance they needed to do to be absolved—some prayers, some charity. Over previous centuries popes had come to proclaim that anyone who made a certain contribution would thereby receive an "indulgence" automatically fulfilling any penance a priest had prescribed. The indulgence might even transfer the merit acquired in this way to a soul suffering in the afterlife but not irretrievably damned. The obvious potential for abuse, the short-circuiting of the necessity for moral and spiritual renewal, were widely criticized, but the financial benefits to the papacy and to rulers who got a portion of the funds raised in their territories, were irresistible. The sale of indulgences, begun in 1515, was intended to raise funds for the building of Saint Peter's in Rome, which to this day impresses many visitors as having a rather doubtful relation to Christian humility.

In 1517 Luther sent his bishop ninety-five theses questioning the lack of any New Testament support for the sale of indulgences. Legend notwithstanding, he did not nail them to the door of the church, but they quickly became known. Somehow they were leaked, possibly by Luther himself, more probably by someone at the bishop's court, translated from Luther's Latin into German, printed, and reprinted in one town after another. Luther had touched a nerve, not only of Christian anger at commercialization of a key moral act but of German anger at papal financial exactions. From the beginning Luther's effectiveness was vastly magnified by the printing press, and he soon became very astute about its uses. The Chinese, of course, had been printing books for four hundred years. The development of printing with movable type in Europe, usually attributed to Johann Gutenberg in 1463, had its indisputably enormous effects first in synergy with the polarizations and mobilizations set off by Luther. Luther himself wrote that printing was "God's highest and extremest act of grace, whereby the business of the gospel is driven forward."[6]

Once Luther's challenge was in print, the supporters of papal policy had to answer it. They tended not to answer effectively Luther's use of the New Testament, but to assert the authority of the positions the church had arrived at in its development of tradition and of the pope as their authoritative interpreter. Between 1517 and 1521 there were several waves of blasts and counter-blasts in print. Luther had two great face-to-face debates with representatives of the papacy. (For the second he walked from Wittenberg to Augsburg and back, a round trip of about 600 miles.) The tone was not genteel. The polarization of defenders and critics of the papacy in and out of the church grew steadily. Defenders of the papacy did not see how reliable unity of teaching and sacraments could be maintained without the accumulated authority of the teachings of the church and the final authority of the present pope.

But Luther insisted that the good Christian could find all the authority he needed in the plain words of the New Testament, especially in the drama of the life, death, and resurrection of Jesus Christ. No hierarchy of priestly intermediaries was necessary; true Christians, he said, formed a "priesthood of all believers." He wrestled with the mysteries of God and man in the New Testament: "For the righteousness of God is revealed from faith to faith, for the righteous shall live by faith" (Romans 1:17). But no weak human being, he feared, could be righteous enough to deserve God's mercy. No, that was the point, righteousness was God's gift to man, in the life, death, and resurrection of his son, and that alone, not anything man could do, made righteousness possible. The world was full of the works of the devil, nowhere more than in the Church of Rome. The only righteousness that could prevail against those dark powers was the gift of God.

In 1521 Luther appeared before Emperor Charles and the Diet of the Holy Roman Empire at Worms, and refused to back down from any of his views: "Here I stand: I can do no other."[7] On his way back to Wittenberg, he was taken captive by friendly forces and held safely incognito in Wartburg castle, where he worked furiously on his German translation of the New Testament. According to the traditional stories, the devil threw walnuts at the ceiling, and he threw an inkwell at the devil. Later in the year, back in Wittenberg where the local prince protected him, he began a long struggle to create a Christian society without the old structures of the Church of Rome. He wrote a great deal. Everything he wrote was published and republished across Europe. He was dismayed by the conclusions others drew from his attacks on Roman authority and his insistence that each Christian should read the New Testament for himself or herself. Even villages were asserting the right to choose their own ministers on their own terms. The people of the village of Wendelstein announced, in a declaration to their pastor, "And so we will recognize you not as a lord but as a servant of the community...and hereby command you to preach the gospel and the Word of God in a pure, clear, and veracious manner."[8] When peasants rose against their oppressors in 1525, he took the side of established authority and does not seem to have flinched at the brutality of the rulers' suppression of the revolts. He married, not nearly as quickly as some other ex-priests, and apparently quite happily.

By the time Luther died in 1546, some version of his teachings was supported by local rulers in many parts of Germany and in Denmark and Sweden. Others had gone further than he in breaking with Rome, the Anabaptists in rejecting infant baptism, and the followers of John Calvin breaking more decisively with old forms of worship and developing a pattern of church government that gave authority to laymen as well as clergy. Luther had gone a long way toward denying the special

MARTINVS LVTHERVS ISLEBIVS
stercoreus Theologus. *et Propheta*.

Pestis eram viuus, moriens ero mors tua Papa:
I nunc, & Christum, te, super ipse loea.
M. D. XLVI.

The determined face of Martin Luther was portrayed many times in the torrent of printings of his works and other Protestant writings. Images like this would have been in many Protestant homes. Library of Congress.

authority of a hierarchy of priests and insisting that every Christian was a priest, making his own way to salvation through his faith in God's mercy. But the churches that followed his teachings still had bishops and were respectful of the non-church authorities.

John Calvin and his associates went much further, insisting that Christians ought to join as equals to create their own godly authority and select their ministers and their civil rulers. Beginning in the 1540s they got a chance to try their ideas out in the city-state of Geneva, in modern Switzerland. The city was governed by a council of ministers and laymen. Enforcement of "godly" standards of conduct was harsh and thorough. The spectacle and ceremony of traditional church services was replaced by long sermons in churches bare of all decoration. In his sermons and writings, Calvin wrestled with a sense of unworthy man confronting an all-powerful God. He could not avoid the conclusion that man could do nothing to save himself, that all depended on God's grace and power. But for Calvin and his followers this was not cause for despair, but for a continuing focus on each individual in an earnest quest for assurance of God's grace in his or her life.

The social and political implications of Calvinism were far more radical than for Lutheranism; people had to take matters in their own hands. They did so as Scotland turned Calvinist, as Englishmen pushed for "puritan" reforms inside and outside their national Church of England, and as the people of modern Belgium and the Netherlands began the riotous destruction of church images and stained glass in 1566; the great medieval churches of the Netherlands still have bare walls, very different from churches that remained Catholic. The Dutch went on to build a new society to which Calvinist moral intensity and individual searching were basic elements. And everywhere, the insistence that each Christian should read the Bible and make basic decisions for himself or herself had led to intense emotions, of the worthlessness of the sinner, the saving power of Jesus's sacrifice, and the terrifying power of the devil, who often worked through witches. By 1700, ordinary people in a few places like the Netherlands and a few wise thinkers elsewhere were beginning to conclude that the only way out of the dreadful conflicts of religious war and persecution was to seek ways in which people of different faiths could respect each other and live side by side in peace.

It is easy to be appalled by Calvin's logic or by Luther's vehement attacks on those who disagreed with him. But Calvin in his sermons was a cautious and caring pastor. Some find in the vast quantity of Luther's writings that the best passages are about spiritual communion with God. Perhaps the best summary of the man and his struggle with what he saw as the forces of evil is found in his great hymn, still sung: "Ein feste Burg ist unser Gott....A mighty fortress is our God....But still our ancient foe does seek to work us woe. His craft and power are great, and armed with cruel hate. On earth is not his equal."

Luther had used the same words "craft and power" for the debating style of an eminent cardinal in 1519, and by then he was well on his way to seeing the pope as the antichrist. For many years loyal Catholics had widely voiced the criticisms of abuses and corruption within the church with which Luther had begun before his break with the Roman Catholic Church. For Catholics, the struggle for survival seemed more urgent than ever as big chunks of Europe were more or less permanently lost to Lutheranism and Calvinism. But it was not until the 1540s that the Church of Rome managed to mount a major reform effort. The Council of Trent, which met intermittently from 1545 to 1563, made systematic plans to reorganize the administration of the church, forbid abuses, and improve clerical education. But it devoted most of its time and energy to questions of church doctrine, seeking authoritative uniformity where there long had been great variety, and shunning any influence of the "heresies" of Luther and Calvin.

Efforts to reform and revive Roman Catholicism included many revivals of discipline in monastic orders and founding new societies and congregations, associations of priests and nuns living under special rules, and coordinating their efforts across wide areas. The great Spanish mystic St. Teresa of Avila, who revived the discipline of her Carmelite order of nuns, founded new convents, and navigated very astutely a world in which women who took initiative and women who talked about God were viewed with grave suspicion.

The most distinctive organizational product of the Catholic Reformation, still a very active presence in the world of today, was the Society of Jesus, the Jesuits. Its founder, Saint Ignatius Loyola had been an airhead young hidalgo, a courtier and brawler, until he got a chance to join in an actual war and saw his leg shattered by a French cannonball. With no courtly romances to read during his long convalescence in the family castle, he turned to religious books and changed his life. Not at all well educated, he sat on benches with pre-adolescent schoolboys to get his Latin up to speed. He set out for Rome, hoping to find a way to join a crusade to Palestine, sometimes reduced to begging, always talking about God to anyone who would listen. He continued to do so as he studied first at Spanish universities and then at the University of Paris. In Paris he gathered about him a small band of followers and began to work out the distinctive way of teaching that is found in his Spiritual Exercises.

Loyola's teaching showed little interest in the deeply private visions of the mystics, but focused on a very exact set of visualizations of the life, death, and resurrection of Jesus Christ and of the decision each Catholic must make to march under Christ's banner. In 1538 the pope recognized Loyola's followers as a new order, the Society of Jesus, owing faithful obedience to the pope and all his successors. The Jesuits soon were active running rigorous, first-class schools for young men, especially of the upper classes, serving as confessors of Catholic princes, and in general working on the front lines of the long struggle to win Europe back for Rome, one prince at a time, or at least to stop the drift to Protestantism and indifference. The Jesuits also had a great vocation as missionaries, and we who study the early modern world are immensely in the debt of these well-educated and sharp-eyed observers of the Amazon, the Sonora Desert, south India, Beijing, Kyoto, and much more.

Revivals and recyclings of great traditions were everywhere. The pilgrimage to Mecca often sent the pilgrim home full of zeal to purify Islamic practice. Tibetan Buddhism, with its emphasis on the reincarnation of successions of lamas (monastic leaders) and even of rulers offered a vivid image of constant renewal of teaching and religious power. Tibetan Buddhism had begun to spread among the Mongols in the days when they ruled China, and in the 1570s a lama declared that Altan Khan, the dominant Mongol lord of that time, was a reincarnation of the mighty Chinggis Khan. Altan in turn bestowed on the lama the title Dalai Lama, "Cosmic Ocean Lama."

A settlement of religious Jews at Safed on the Sea of Galilee renewed their faith through studies focused on the Kabbalah, a kind of interpretation, not altogether unlike those of the Sufis and very interesting to some Christians, that found hidden meaning and numerical correspondences in sacred texts. Their greatest teacher, Isaac Luria, developed a profound theory of how the perfection of God and his creation had been lost, but still fragments of the divine light were everywhere; the good Jew was obliged to pursue a goal of *tikkun*, restoration of that wholeness, the end of the exile suffered not just by Jews but by all humanity, through worship and moral action. One is reminded of Wang Gen's dream of putting back the falling heavens.

Renewals are long-run changes and do not fit very neatly into a 1530–1570 time frame. Several key figures actually were contemporaries of Columbus. (Machiavelli, Sri Krishna Caitanya, Wang Yangming, and Martin Luther). Each trend began before 1450, made some pretty dramatic changes between then and 1530, and continued to echo in minds and hearts long after. The gulfs among the cultures were enormous. Machiavelli and Luther would not have had anything to say to Caitanya or Wang, nor Caitanya and Wang to each other. But from our distance, we can see some parallels. All these movements were the creations of men who were very well educated in their great textual traditions and could draw on the accumulated editions and interpretations of many generations of devoted scholars. All drew easily on classical texts in their own writings. But they also felt the dead hand of accumulated erudition and reasoning, and struggled to free themselves from it and to focus on the experience, the emotion, at the heart of what had been recorded. The turn to individual experience opened the way, to a greater or lesser degree, to pay attention to the evidence of the senses and to new ideas. The ordinary devotee, without erudition or class standing, was a full participant who did not have to defer to the received ideas of his betters. Printing helped to spread new personal views in Europe and perhaps in China. Hindus responded in different ways to the intrusion of Islam in their world. Luther and the merchants and intellectuals of Venice and Florence were thoroughly aware of the rising Ottoman power. The Chinese of Wang Yangming's time did not feel threatened by Islam, but were still working out the effects of the shock of Mongol rule over their world two hundred years before. Merchants, towns, and big assemblies of people enhanced these movements in different mixes. Most of all, these astonishing transformations through revivals of ancient heritages serve to remind every student of history that the hand of the past need not be dead, but a source of fresh life for the human mind and spirit.

New Shapes of Power, 1570–1610

In 1694 Sir Josiah Child, at that time the dominant figure in the English East India Company, wrote, "Trade does contribute in a very great measure to the honor, strength, wealth, and preservation of our government."[1] The idea that there can be a synergy of profit and power, that increase of private wealth and profit, and increase of the coercive power of the state can, indeed must, support each other and interact positively, is a commonplace today. Rulers who do not facilitate the growth of their national economies lose legitimacy almost as quickly as those who are bullied by other countries. Strong economies are in themselves sources of the "soft power" of aid, commercial expansion, and cultural influence, and they pay for military power.

The possibility that profit and power could support each other was not commonplace in the world of 1450; it would be quite a bit more widely understood and pursued by 1700. Englishmen, Frenchmen, Spaniards, and many others had been arguing about the best policies to produce private wealth and national strength since the early 1500s. At several times in China's long history, statesmen had pursued *fuguo qiangbing (fu guoh chiahng bing)*, a rich state and a strong military, but this was definitely wealth in the service of power and not vice versa. Venice and Genoa had battled for centuries before 1400 for domination of the profitable trades of the eastern Mediterranean. Shifting diplomatic alliances, the pursuit of profit and power together, the possibilities and limits of exploiting a conquest, all were highly developed in the statecraft of Renaissance Italy. This statecraft spread to northern Europe as a coherent nation-state system developed, and states adopted "mercantilist" policies. These were measures that were supposed to promote profit-power synergies by giving a monopoly of a line of trade or of the right to produce certain luxury goods to the nation's own businessmen.

But to the statesmen of the "gunpowder empires," Ottoman, Safavid, and Mughal, it seemed that prosperity and commercial profit were likely to lead to political instability and loss of power. One difficulty was that so many of the most adept merchants and artisans were not

Muslim—Hindus in the Mughal empire, Armenians in the Safavid, Armenians and Greeks in the Ottoman. Also, high taxes could endanger stability in a very large and diverse empire; dissident provincial leaders could tap new wealth.

The Chinese empire faced similar contradictions with different strategies for preserving unity and stability. Japan was another matter; starting about 1450 it transformed itself into an immensely dynamic sphere of competing realms, passed through a century of intense and dangerous interaction with the outside world, then limited foreign contacts and imposed a remarkable domestic peace, but preserved the profit-power competitiveness of the many realms within its borders. Its history offers rich food for thought about state systems and the synergies of profit and power.

Japan's political tradition had as one of its basic principles the unbroken hereditary continuity of the imperial line, descended from the Sun Goddess. But since about 800 the emperors had not been expected to rule actively, but rather to legitimize the power of others. From about 1100, these others were *samurai* warriors, and the leader of the most powerful coalition of samurai was named *shogun*, or general, and was a military dictator over the whole country. There were times when this system provided a reasonably stable order, but by 1450 it had unraveled into chaos. In 1467 there were full-scale battles among rival samurai forces in the streets of Kyoto, the capital and residence of the powerless emperor. These battles shattered a fragile set of arrangements for ruling outlying regions, so that local contenders fought for dominance in every region. Here and there a samurai leader who had a stronger base than others in local land-holding and was smarter and luckier than others began to build a more stable structure and consolidate a territorial base; *daimyo* was the term for regional lords from this time down to the 1800s.

The magnitude of the change the daimyo made in Japan's political order can be seen in comments by foreign eyewitnesses just forty years apart. About 1580 a Jesuit missionary with long experience of Japan wrote that the Japanese "rebel against [the rulers] whenever they have a chance.... Then they turn and declare themselves friends again, only to rebel once more when the opportunity presents itself." In 1620, an equally well-informed English merchant in Japan wrote that the government of Japan "may well be accounted the greatest and most powerful tyranny that ever was heard of in the world, for all the rest are as slaves to the emperor, or great commander as they call him," so that anyone whom the ruler suspected of disloyalty would commit suicide if ordered to do so.[2] The Jesuit was writing at the height of what the Japanese call the "age of warring realms," with larger and more destructive armies fighting each other every year, with vassals rebelling against their lords and several kinds of religious extremists rebelling against all worldly authority. By the time the Englishman wrote, the shogun, the "emperor or great commander" of whom he wrote, was an heir to the founder of the house of Tokugawa that would rule Japan until 1868. There was no large-scale opposition to his rule. Many daimyo, including some who had fought against the Tokugawa, were secure in control of provincial realms as long as they did not challenge the larger structure. Peace, prosperity, and hierarchical stability were doing their work. Later in the 1600s Japan was one of the most prosperous, and almost certainly the most orderly, place in the world.

Compared with the disorders of the same times in Europe, the Japanese collapse into chaos seems quicker and more complete, with fewer survivals of urban and local structures. But Japan's shift to creation of new forms of order also was amazingly swift; Japan's disorders were over in the mid-1600s, while Europe's still were bottoming out. The fragility of the old order that collapsed around 1450 was offset by a background awareness of the importance of settled bureaucratic administration and record-keeping, inherited from the Chinese tradition by way of the medieval Japanese state. Astute daimyo, in between plots, ambushes, and every form of warrior derring-do, established courts that decided among rival claims to land and proclaimed their own law codes of local conduct. None of this was authorized by higher authority, which scarcely existed, but to the degree local people accepted it, the daimyo's power and legitimacy grew steadily.

The great changes that began in the late 1500s were partly the work of three men who expanded the power and strategies of the daimyo—super-daimyo on a Japan-wide stage. But they were just the top layer of a profound struggle for order. The chaos of the late 1500s was not just a matter of coalitions of samurai fighting each other; peasants organized in self-defense, and especially when inspired by the teachings of some Buddhist sect—or soon, Roman Catholicism—they formed powerful communities that rejected samurai dominance entirely. The first super-daimyo, Oda Nobunaga, crushed these alternative forms of organization, especially when he savagely attacked the warrior monks of the great Hieizan Buddhist monastery complex outside Kyoto in 1571.

Nobunaga built his power primarily by building the largest and best military alliance and crushing his enemies; it was fairly predictable that some of them would catch him off guard, and he was assassinated in 1582. Among his able commanders was one of the most important and unusual figures in the history of the early modern world, Toyotomi Hideyoshi. Tiny, ugly, of humble rural origin, Hideyoshi was one of many daimyo allied with Nobunaga. After Nobunaga's assassination, he was in a position to move quickly to take control of Kyoto and to begin building his own alliances.

Soon Hideyoshi showed a political style very different from that of his former master. Where Nobunaga had crushed his defeated enemies, Hideyoshi co-opted them, assuring them of survival and a territory with a good income if they would join him and perhaps accept a move to a different base area. To many daimyo, cooperating with him as an equal seemed preferable to subordination to Nobunaga's surviving sons. A defeated enemy might not only survive but be rewarded for participation in the next campaign. There were many battles, many dangerous moments, and some very harsh assaults on armed Buddhist sects. But the warfare of the time was not all ambush and sword-fighting; contacts with the Portuguese had brought the musket to Japan. Many samurai, and Hideyoshi more than anyone, understood that effective use of this formidable new weapon required disciplined infantry forces and good connections with the merchants who supplied the lead and gunpowder. In a daimyo's realm, peace, prosperity, and trade were essential to the new kind of warfare.

By 1587 Hideyoshi and his allies were in control of the main island, Honshu, and ready to invade Kyushu, where his broadening alliance soon subdued and co-opted the powerful local daimyo. Portuguese and Chinese traders came to the ports of Kyushu, and the local daimyo controlled a thriving trade with the Ryukyu Islands to the south. Daimyo who wanted to attract the Portuguese had been hospitable to the missionaries who had accompanied them, and by this time there were some communities of fervent Catholic converts on the island and even a few convert daimyo. To Hideyoshi and many others, they looked much too much like the Buddhist sects who had challenged samurai dominance and had been crushed; the turn against the Christian presence began in 1587 with a prohibition of efforts to spread Catholicism and a threat to expel the missionaries, and turned to brutal suppression in the early 1600s. Hideyoshi also began a system of licensing and controlling foreign trade in Japanese ships.

For years Hideyoshi had had big visions for what he might accomplish in Japan, establishing a long-lasting peace. He now went a long way to make that vision reality and to make the world safe and secure for daimyo and samurai who would play their proper roles in his system. In 1588 he forbade the possession of swords by farmers; the samurai who searched out and confiscated all the weapons kept meticulous inventories. In 1591 samurai were forbidden to live in peasant villages, so that they would not have a base for individual action in control of peasant manpower and taxes. The status of each individual was determined by birth and meticulously recorded.

Swords, the world's best swords, were the mark of samurai rank. But samurai could not use them to rule or mobilize a peasant community. As salaried officers of a daimyo, they had secure status and income but no autonomy. Unique among the armed elites of early modern times, they had no direct control over the products of peasant labor, but lived near the castle of a daimyo and drew a salary from the taxes they collected from villages in their individual domains.

Merchants and craftsmen could not wear swords, but daimyo and their samurai agents understood that trade brought prosperity that could support military strength. The daimyo sought to attract merchants and craftsmen to settle near the daimyo castle. The daimyo could be moved or theoretically even dismissed by Hideyoshi, but he was secure from challenge from below by autonomous samurai, and the samurai had nothing to fear either from weapon-wielding peasants or from organized and armed religious sects. In the 1590s the whole structure of local rule was documented in meticulous surveys of amounts of land, the taxes for which they were liable, and the numbers of samurai warriors a daimyo was obliged to support in return for receiving this revenue. These were the foundations of the amazing recovery from civil war and social chaos since 1550, and of the order that gave Japan internal peace until after 1800 and laid the foundations for its distinctive roles in the world of the nineteenth and twentieth centuries.

The foundations of Hideyoshi's regime lay in superior force, and the last two centuries of war had shown how quickly that could vanish. Hideyoshi, with none of the claims to descent from the great medieval aristocrats and warrior houses that could help legitimize his rule, sought an unusually close relation with the imperial court, arranging to be granted and known by civilian court titles, not the military title of shogun, and building his own great mansion in Kyoto, the imperial capital. A great outdoor festival in the fall of 1587 when Hideyoshi and the capital aristocracy mingled with the most refined performers of the tea ceremony, with their elaborate procedures and exquisitely rare utensils, and the magnificent procession when the emperor himself came to visit Hideyoshi's mansion in 1588, were two moments when his statecraft and stagecraft were the equal of anything at the courts of his contemporaries, Queen Elizabeth of England and Akbar, the Mughal emperor.

With Kyushu in hand and connections opened up with a wider world, Hideyoshi developed some astonishing projects for domination of that world. His forces would invade Korea, march into China, and install the Japanese emperor in Beijing as universal ruler. His hardened armies would have no problem with the mountains of the Korean peninsula; they were among the world's best mountain fighters. Not incidentally, he would give the daimyo of Kyushu, including the Catholics, chances to prove their military merit and to win huge new rewards as his allies. Still, the megalomania of this vision, and the contrast with Japan's caution about involvement with the Asian mainland through most of its history, are amazing and baffling even to specialists in the period.

In 1592 an army of about a hundred thousand samurai crossed the straits to Korea and advanced rapidly to capture the capital, Seoul, from which the ill-prepared Korean army fled. But as the Japanese forces continued north, they encountered growing guerrilla resistance. Korean admiral Yi Sun Shin supervised the building of a fleet of so-called turtle ships, with armor plates and covered decks, which harried supply lines between Japan and its armies in Korea. The rulers of Ming China made sure of good relations with the formidable rulers of the Jurchen people, on the northeast frontiers of China and to the north of Korea, and sent an expedition to oppose Hideyoshi. He withdrew to the far south of the peninsula, negotiations started and stopped, war broke out again, and when Hideyoshi died in 1598, his generals quickly completed their withdrawal.

Hideyoshi did not manage to legitimize the inheritance of his power by his son. In 1600 two great coalitions of daimyo fought a decisive battle at Sekigahara, and the forces led by Tokugawa Ieyasu won. Tokugawa quickly obtained imperial appointment as shogun and began building his base of power at Edo, modern Tokyo, until then a small town but in an area rich in agricultural and fishing resources and crucial connections to the north. Hideyoshi's heir and his supporters were not eliminated at that time; but in 1615, as anti-Tokugawa forces mobilized very dangerously around the heir, Tokugawa summoned all his allies and crushed their enemies, destroying their base at Osaka Castle. The descendants of Tokugawa Ieyasu ruled Japan as shogun until 1868, in one of the most singularly organized, peaceful, and prosperous parts of the early modern world. Their political order built on Hideyoshi's foundations; daimyo might be moved to a new territory, but even those who had opposed Ieyasu at Sekigahara were allowed to keep a territory and samurai somewhere.

All daimyo had years of hard work ahead of them, getting full control of their territories and their samurai. In the early years they tried to concentrate as much wealth and power as possible because it seemed likely that civil war would break out again. The long peace that followed brought new financial pressures. Daimyo were expected to keep some of their samurai in residence at Edo at all times and to spend alternate years there themselves. Living there, and moving themselves and their retainers back and forth, was a very expensive business. Great mansions, splendid gardens, exquisite silk kimonos, refined porcelain, and marvelous theatricals were necessary and expensive parts of the Edo high life. Trying to promote prosperity in their realms, daimyo and their samurai built up well-organized towns full of shops and fine craft production around their castles. In the late 1600s five of the twenty largest cities in the world were in Japan. Edo grew in its first century into one of the world's great cities.

In the 1630s the Tokugawa rulers became convinced that foreign trade was dangerous to political stability and had to be severely limited and controlled. The Catholic missionaries and their Portuguese merchant associates were expelled, and Japanese Christians were treated with great brutality. Japanese were forbidden to go abroad. The Dutch and the Chinese were allowed strictly limited, supervised trade at Nagasaki on Kyushu. The authorities kept a very careful watch on this trade, and they questioned every arriving captain about events in the world. This isolated watchful waiting and thorough control of foreign contacts lasted with only small modifications until Perry's American "Black Ships" arrived in 1853 and began to force Japan to open to the world.

We are more familiar with the shapes of profit and power in Europe than with those in Japan. "Profit and power" was a slogan of an English merchant-statesman, and the pursuit of this synergy was a great English success story, which also involved some melodramas of court life as lurid as anything in Japan. If a knowledgeable European in 1450 had been asked to name the continent's great centers of wealth and power, he might have mentioned Rome, Florence, Venice, Prague, Nuremberg, Antwerp, or Paris, certainly not London or Amsterdam. But by 1650 or 1700 those cities were the centers of great military and naval powers with worldwide networks of trade and vital and innovative cultures. The rise of England and of the Dutch United Provinces are the best-studied cases of profit and power interacting to create the modern world; Sir Josiah Child of the English East India Company was a Englishman trying to figure out how his country could catch up with the Dutch.

England in 1450 was constantly torn apart by the wars of its great noble houses, each fighting to put its own man on the royal throne. The country had not been a great center of urban finance and production in the previous centuries, but it was a supplier of a basic agricultural commodity, wool. By 1450 it was far along in a shift from providing raw wool for weaving and finishing in continental Europe to doing its own weaving and finishing for export, and thus keeping more of the profits from its raw materials at home. But England desperately needed political stability. That came in 1485, when a final turn in the civil wars among the great feudal houses brought to the throne Henry Tudor, Henry VII. Cautious and shrewd, Henry married a lady from the opposite side of the wars, so that his son would have the loyalty of both sides, and consolidated central power. His son and his granddaughter were Henry VIII (reigned 1509–1547) and Elizabeth I (reigned 1558–1603), masters of royal showmanship in an age when statecraft and stagecraft were even more closely linked than usual. The melodramas of the private life of Henry VIII (two queens divorced, two executed, one who died giving birth to the only son who outlived him, one who outlived him) can distract us from the far-reaching political changes of his reign. Not much interested in the details of government, Henry was an unlikely catalyst for such major changes.

If the consolidation of royal power begun by his father was to continue beyond his death, he had to have a legitimate child surviving him, and a son would be much safer. (England could be ruled by a queen, but many would be tempted to defy her, assuming that she was not a warrior or fit to command.) In 1525 Henry's queen, Catherine of Aragon, was forty, and not likely to have more children. Their only living child was a daughter. The king had his eye on the young Anne Boleyn. He sought an annulment by the pope of his marriage to Catherine to open the way to a fully legitimate Catholic marriage to Anne. The influence of Catherine's relatives, the rulers of Spain, blocked the annulment. Henry, who had written a tract defending the pope against Martin Luther's attacks, was plunged into the break with Rome by the imperatives of hereditary monarchy.

He secured from church authorities in England the annulment and marriage, just in time to make legitimate the birth to Queen Anne Boleyn in 1533 of a child. At the same time he convened a parliament that was encouraged to vent popular feelings against the wealth and corruption of the church. His hope, apparently, was that the pope would be intimidated into approving the annulment and marriage after the fact. The pope refused. The child was a girl, named Elizabeth. The pope excommunicated Henry, and Henry and his parliament broke the last ties of the Church of England to Rome, declaring the English monarch the supreme head of the Church of England; this continues today. In 1535 the king's agents fanned out across the kingdom to investigate corruption of all kinds in the monasteries, with a great deal of enthusiastic help from ordinary people, and the vast properties of the monasteries were confiscated, about 20 percent to 25 percent of the kingdom. The king collected rent from these lands, granted some of them to loyal and meritorious supporters, and eventually sold many of them.

This vast increase in royal power and wealth could have set the stage for a permanent gain in power concentrated in the hands of the king or queen and a few ministers. In fact, it opened the way to new forms of interaction and power-sharing between the crown and elite. The king and his ministers learned a great deal about managing parliament in encouraging the attacks on the monasteries and pushing through the many parliamentary bills required for the changes in the church. The king was unable or unwilling to live within the income he got from rents on monasteries and other royal lands, and in the 1540s large amounts of land were sold at bargain rates. The buyers were not often great nobles, but people of moderate means investing in them in hope of building their fortunes. These changes created a broader landed elite who owed a great deal to the monarchy. They carried on their quarrels with their neighbors not with private armies, as they had a hundred years before, but in the courts of law and in the endless chess game of access to the royal person.

The king used some of his greatly increased income to buy fancy clothes and build dazzling palaces, but more of it to pay for expanded fleets and armies and to intervene in wars on the continent. England was not yet a key player in those wars, in which the Holy Roman Empire and France sought to dominate Italy, but it was a valued and sought-after ally.

The new landholders often converted plowed fields into sheep pastures, providing wool for the still-growing export trade. The growth of trade and of London and other cities, the frantic search for wealth, the plight of farmers evicted from their tenant holdings in favor of sheep, set off vehement debates, in print and in Parliament, about the "commonwealth," about ways in which government policy affected people's livelihoods. Some of the people involved had experience as merchants or otherwise were adept at exact quantitative reasoning about prices, the effects of currency devaluations, and much more. Merchants, craftsmen, and landowners everywhere had and have well-developed ideas about how the government can encourage a just and prosperous economy; however, making these matters public and giving non-officials some chance to influence government policies was very unusual and very much a product of the political melodramas of the court of Henry VIII.

Henry's Church of England did not diverge very much from Roman Catholic teaching and ceremony, but all the radical teachings from the continent, from Luther to Calvin and beyond, now could find a hearing within the English church and society without interference from Rome. After Henry's death in 1547, the government of the boy king Edward VI veered sharply toward Protestantism. But then under Henry's daughter Mary, who reigned from 1553 to 1558, a real effort was made to force England back into obedience to the Roman Catholic Church, and several hundred defiant Protestants were burned at the stake. When Elizabeth, daughter of Henry VIII and Anne Boleyn, came to the throne in 1558, a continuation of the polarization and violence of the previous ten years seemed likely. And many were sure that a queen could not be a strong ruler.

But Elizabeth, with the help of some remarkably able ministers, maintained stability and oversaw a remarkable rise of England as a European power, the beginnings of English overseas trade to the eastern Mediterranean, Russia, Africa, the Americas, and the Indian Ocean, and the dramatic defeat of the Spanish Armada sent to invade England in 1588. She was quite learned, a superb performer on the stage of her court, a maker of wonderful speeches, and a most astute politician. It was essential to her politics, and to the image that so enthralled her people, that she never married. To marry in that age would be to submit herself to a superior; to marry a member of another royal house would be to bind herself to her husband's family interests. The principles and practices for the Church of England that she crafted with her ministers and parliaments moved away from many features of Roman Catholicism, but not too far or too fast, and left room for "Puritans" who wanted a more thorough break with the Catholic heritage to think they might still get their way within the Church of England. The beauties of the Book of Common Prayer spoke to many then, and still do today: "Lighten our darkness, we beseech Thee, O Lord; and by thy great mercy defend us from all perils and dangers of this night; for the love of thy only Son, our Savior Jesus Christ."[3]

England's "commonwealth" under Elizabeth was shaped by the interests of a wide class of prosperous men whose fortunes had their origins in trade, in the bargain purchase of monastery lands from her father, and in a long general expansion of trade and prosperity in her reign. Entrepreneurs with ideas about how to make money out of a new trade connection sought from the royal court grants of some kind of monopoly privilege that would protect the new and fragile businesses; others might add their funds to such an enterprise, and even the queen bought shares in what were

Elizabeth Regina.

2. PARALIPOM. 6.

q Domine Deus Israell, non est similis tui Deus in cælo & in terr, qui pacta custodis & misericordiam cum seruis tuis, qui ã bulant coram te in toto corde suo.

Queen Elizabeth I of England kneels in prayer, her scepter and sword laid aside. But the royal coat of arms and the splendid fabrics that surround her make this a figure of power. Courtesy of the Rare Book and Special Collections Library, University of Illinois at Urbana-Champaign, 248 D33b 1581.

appropriately called "adventures." English merchants sailed around the North Cape of Norway, traded with Russia and even across it to the silk trade center at Astrakhan on the Caspian Sea; probed trade possibilities on the west coast of Africa; traded and raided in the Caribbean, in defiance of Spanish claims of monopoly; tried but failed to establish a colony on the coast of what is now North Carolina; and at the very end of the reign organized the East India Company that would monopolize English trade east of the Cape of Good Hope.

Philip V of Spain was among the marriage suitors whom Elizabeth had refused, and in European politics England threw its weight against the great power of Spain, sending troops in the 1580s to assist the Dutch rebels against Spain. In 1588, with superb seamanship, a great deal of luck, and a convenient storm at sea, the English defeated the Spanish Armada, a great fleet that was to have convoyed a big Spanish army from the Netherlands to invade England. It was one of the most famous moments in English history and one of the great triumphs of profit and power in world history. Queen Elizabeth had spoken to the troops assembled to defend England against the Spanish invasion: "My loving people, We have been persuaded by some that are careful of our safety, to take heed of how we commit ourselves to armed multitudes, for fear of treachery [That is, some had advised her not to go out to speak to the troops.]; but I assure you that I do not desire to live to distrust my faithful and loving people. Let tyrants fear, I have always placed my chiefest strength and safeguard in the loyal hearts and good-will of my subjects....I know I have the body but of a weak and feeble woman; but I have the heart and stomach of a king, and a king of England too, and think foul scorn that Parma [the Spanish commander] or any prince of Europe, should dare to invade the borders of my realm."[4] The Queen's "royal we" and her stunning play on her "weakness" as a woman were sources of national strength not available to all monarchs, and even less to leaders of new states less focused on a ruler, such as the Netherlands.

In the early 1500s the Low Countries, especially in cities like Antwerp and Bruges in modern Belgium, were great centers of commercial wealth, with long-established privileges of autonomous rule by local elites. As a result of a long sequence of marriages and inheritances, the Hapsburg rulers of Spain were the sovereigns of the area. A long-established trend of individualistic and intense Christian devotion contributed to enthusiastic local responses to the messages of Luther and Calvin, and equally vehement repressions by the Spanish rulers and the Catholic authorities. Urban leaders and local nobles joined in resistance to Spanish efforts to impose tighter control, Spanish troops were sent, and in 1567 the astute local noble William of Orange led others in open revolt and the expulsion of the Spanish garrisons.

From 1579 to 1581 the cities and provinces of the northern Netherlands declared themselves an independent and sovereign union. William of Orange, often called William the Silent, was named *stadholder*, literally administrator of the state, chief administrator, and commander in chief, but he and his descendants remained formally appointees of the government of the United Provinces, not its rulers. In each province, such as Zeeland and Holland, the various cities appointed representatives to a provincial assembly, and in turn each province appointed representatives to the national assembly, the Estates

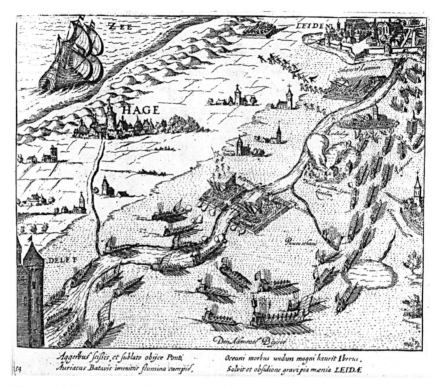

Aggeribus fæßis, et fublato obijce Ponti,
Furiatus Batavis immittit flumina campis,

Oceani morens undam magni haurit Iberus.
Solvit et obfidione gravi pia mænia LEIDÆ.

The Dutch have cut some dikes, the rain falls, and as water spreads across the flat Dutch fields in 1574 the troops of William of Orange arrive to drive off the Spanish forces besieging Leiden. The Dutch remained masters of their fragile landscape and their own future. Library of Congress, LC-USZ62-60379.

General. At each level the representative often had to stick strictly to the instructions he had been given and to seek new orders when new situations came up. Although it was the Estates General that appointed and instructed diplomats and made decisions of war and peace, many people thought real sovereignty was at the level of the provinces or even the cities.

But the whole ramshackle business worked. William was an astute politician, and as his son Maurice came to maturity around 1600, he proved to be a military genius. The United Provinces had ample financial resources from their trade, and they were fighting for their lives. Amsterdam's prosperity was founded on its position as an entrepot, a port where the widest possible range of goods, from North Sea herring to Spanish salt to Scandinavian timber to Indonesian spices, was readily available. The tax system of the United Provinces was complicated, with many local variations, but effective in its reliance on taxes on sales and other transactions, which were easily collected and placed the burden on the prosperous and growing parts of the economy. The Netherlands proved that profit and power need not depend on a tightly centralized state system, and could be compatible with local autonomy and privilege.

A centralized admiralty built up a superb unified fleet that not only defended the homeland but reached out into the power struggles of the Baltic. A truce with Spain in 1609 was a major step toward formal acceptance of Dutch independence. When a dangerous split developed over foreign policy and religion in 1618, the prestige of Maurice and his position as commander of the armies enabled him to enforce his views and secure the execution of his leading opponent. The truce expired in 1621, more battles were fought, and it was only in 1648 that the United Provinces were permanently recognized as a sovereign nation.

In 1648 to 1650 another potentially dangerous split between supporters of Maurice's successors in the House of Orange and partisans of municipal and provincial autonomy was avoided only by the sudden death of the young stadholder William II. From 1650 to 1672 there was no stadholder, and the merchant elite, especially that of Amsterdam, was fully in charge. In these decades of what the Dutch called their "True Freedom," the Netherlands was Europe's greatest center of publishing. In its religious life there were a wide range of types of Protestantism; a Jewish community, largely exiles from Spain and Portugal, who provided expertise in international trade and the workings of the stock market; and Catholics who were forbidden to hold public services but had splendid chapels discreetly hidden in the attics and corners of fine houses. A broad allegiance to tolerance as a virtue meshed nicely with the practical necessities of a world entrepot.

Disaster came in 1672 with a very dangerous French invasion and the brutal murder by a mob of two leaders of the government. William III, the stadholder who now stepped in, worked effectively with the merchant elite, strengthened his own position, and in a final amazing act of wealth and power organized the successful invasion of England in 1688.

By 1600 Dutchmen were trading everywhere the English were, and they were pushing into the trade of the Indian Ocean. Starting out with individual voyages sent out by different cities and provinces, the Dutch found that in those distant ports they needed to unite to defend themselves against the Portuguese and not compete with each other. In 1602 the Dutch rulers worked out a remarkable mix of localism and centralization, the United Dutch East India Company. It had "chambers" in various cities and provinces. Its governing council had seventeen members. Amsterdam, by far the largest trading city, appointed eight, the province of Zeeland four, lesser chambers one each. So Amsterdam was hugely influential but could do nothing without getting votes from the other chambers. Chambers invested separately in ships and cargoes at the European end, but in Asia the company soon developed a centralized structure, with a governor-general and council at Batavia, modern Jakarta, Indonesia. The Batavia authorities coordinated trade from Japan to Iran, made their own wars and alliances with Asian rulers, and kept remarkable records of all that the Dutch saw and learned in Asian ports.

They also gave real opportunities for advancement of a kind rare anywhere in the world of the 1600s to ambitious poor men who managed to survive the first year or so of tropical diseases. Anthony van Diemen, for example, had failed in business in Amsterdam and was fleeing his creditors when he signed on with the company in 1617. The head of the company's operations in Asia, Governor General Jan Pietersz Coen, was a very able and strong-willed commander who was constantly writing to his superiors in the home country to tell them what he could accomplish if they sent him more ships and men, and who did not hesitate to deal very harshly with Asians who got in his way. He saw van Diemen's abilities and promoted him very rapidly. From 1636 to 1645 van Diemen was governor general of the company's operations in Asia. Very much interested in expanding geographical knowledge and seeking new opportunities for trade, he sent exploratory voyages off to the north and east of Japan, where they found nothing, and to the south and east of Java, where they explored the coasts of New Guinea and Australia but found few opportunities for trade.

When a local ruler gave the company a monopoly to purchase a certain product, like the cloves and nutmeg of eastern Indonesia, its enforcement of that monopoly often was brutal. The small Banda Islands far out in the east of present-day Indonesia were the world's sole source of nutmeg and mace, two costly spices from the same tree, used for flavoring and preservation and traded all the way to Europe. The people of Banda had a wide maritime trade network of their own, and they resisted as best they could while the Dutch built a fort and signed contracts with local headmen who agreed to sell spices only to the Dutch.

No one ruler had the right to commit all the Bandanese to such an arrangement, and the headmen had no experience of such legal complications. In 1621 Coen ordered the forcible occupation of the main islands. Forty Bandanese headmen were executed, many others were enslaved, and the rest were killed in assaults on their villages or died

In Maluku, the "Spice Islands" of eastern Indonesia, forces of the Dutch East India Company allied with and fought against local warriors. Dutch artists captured some vivid images of them, but publication often was delayed by Company fears of information that would aid competitors. KITLV / Royal Institute of Southeast Asian and Caribbean Studies at Leiden.

of hunger and exposure during the rainy season. Very few Bandanese survived even as slaves, and the nutmeg groves were leased to European settlers and the work in them done by slaves bought elsewhere in Asia.

Power was supposed to produce monopoly profits, and in the short run it did. Late in the 1600s the Dutch company still was building new forts to try to enforce its clove monopolies, and was more and more deeply involved in trying to dominate the intricate politics of the big, densely populated island of Java. Neither the Spice Islands nor eastern Java were major sources of goods in growing demand in Europe, and it was no longer clear that the application of power was producing profits for the Dutch company, to say nothing of its impact on the local peoples. But it was, nevertheless, a remarkable case of the building of a centralized power on a decentralized foundation of local privilege. The English company, founded before the Dutch, did not catch up with it as a structure of wealth and power until around 1700, as it became a major player in the trade of the Indian subcontinent, one of the great frontiers of opportunity and plunder of the following century.

The Dutch East India Company spread its power in maritime Southeast Asia in the 1600s, and had complicated relations with a large number of local rulers who also were interested in the positive relationship between profits of trade and military power. The impact of Dutch aggression destroyed some of these rulers and blunted the growth of others, but there were some who continued to grow well beyond 1700. Some were in the middle of rich rice lands, but many were in coastal enclaves surrounded by mountains or mangrove swamps that had plenty

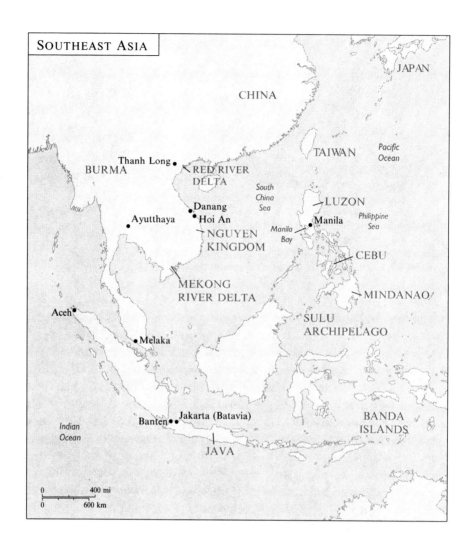

SOUTHEAST ASIA

JAPAN

CHINA

TAIWAN   *Pacific Ocean*

Thanh Long •
BURMA   ⤷ RED RIVER
          DELTA   *South China Sea*

          • Danang   ⤷ LUZON
Ayutthaya • Hoi An   • Manila   *Philippine Sea*
          ⤷ NGUYEN   *Manila Bay*
            KINGDOM   ⤷ CEBU

          • MEKONG
            RIVER DELTA   ⤷ MINDANAO
Aceh •
                         SULU
          • Melaka   ARCHIPELAGO

                              BANDA
          Banten • • Jakarta (Batavia)   ISLANDS
Indian Ocean
          JAVA

0   400 mi
0   600 km

of fish but had to import their rice by sea. Among them were Aceh on
the north end of Sumatra; the kingdom of Ayutthaya in what is now
Thailand; and the Nguyen realm in what is now central Vietnam.

The sultans of Aceh (Ah cheh) rose to power as the champions of
Islam in a region where the Portuguese conquest of Melaka had been
a big setback for Muslim power. They were prominent participants
in most of the Muslim alliances that attacked Portuguese Melaka in
the 1500s. In 1566 the sultan of Aceh sent an appeal for financial and
diplomatic assistance against the Portuguese to the Ottoman sultan in
Istanbul. Aceh had Islamic law courts, and Muslims from Iran and the

Indian subcontinent were numerous and influential among its resident foreign merchants. It reached a peak of wealth and power under Sultan Iskander Muda, who reigned from 1607 to 1636, keeping unusually tight control on all traders and every aspect of life in his capital, and encouraging Islamic learning. Aceh never was on good terms with the Dutch, and after about 1650 the constant hostilities seem to have undercut its wealth and power.

In the great valley of Southeast Asia's Menam River, which flows past the ancient capital of Ayutthaya (Ah yoo tai ya) and modern Bangkok, there seldom was any problem about the food supply; two good rice crops a year were the norm. The kingdom of Ayutthaya was founded about 1350. Its rulers encouraged the ancient Theravada form of Buddhism, which had been especially well preserved in Sri Lanka; it lays great emphasis on monasteries as centers of devotion and education, and, without much challenge to political authority, gives stability and discipline to society. Although rulers rarely managed to name their own successors, so that every succession was a whirlpool of violence and intrigue, good order and prosperity quickly returned.

There was a devastating Burmese invasion in 1568. But the fundamentals of food supply and military manpower were very solid. Ordinary farmers could be called up for service to the rulers for as much as six months a year, the months that were not needed for planting and harvesting all that rice. As in Africa, wealth and power depended more on mobilizing enough labor than it did on controlling land. The Burmese invaders withdrew fairly quickly, taking thousands of captives with them to work their fields.

Local strongmen in the countryside were always working to divert labor from the royal pool to their own purposes, especially when a succession crisis loomed. So the kings needed leverage from outside this system of land and labor. They got it from foreign trade and foreign residents. Chinese traders had settled along the lower Menam for centuries; the founder of the Ayutthaya kingdom is said to have been partly of Chinese ancestry. Resident Chinese, completely bilingual and bicultural, frequently staffed the kingdom's Ministry of Foreign Trade, a major source of royal revenue, and manned and managed the voyages of the king's trading ships to China, Japan, and Java. In the 1600s one powerful family producing many high officials was of Iranian Muslim origin. One king early in the 1600s had a bodyguard of émigré Japanese, whose descendants remained another element in the cultural mix.

The kings and their high officials, secure in their Buddhist practices, in the traditional ceremonies surrounding the king, and in the large armies they could assemble from the villages, saw the foreign traders as convenient sources of revenue and no threat to the security and order of their realm. Ayutthaya made a great impression on foreign visitors, with the great gold-covered statues and towers of its Buddhist temples and the lavishly decorated boats in which the king and his high officials went up and down the river. In the 1680s Ayutthaya was the scene of a political melodrama as the French tried to influence its politics, and a few deluded missionaries hoped to convert the king to Christianity. But the king died, the French were sent away, and the kingdom continued on a fairly even keel into the 1700s.

In the 1600s a powerful little trading state grew up on the central coast of modern Vietnam, not far from Hue, at the port city of Hoi An. This was a regional regime, at first formally under the Le dynasty, which ruled in the area of modern Hanoi. The Le rulers were very dependent on a number of other powerful families of warrior aristocrats, especially the Trinh (Jing), the Nguyen (roughly ngoo en), and the Mac. By 1520 the Mac had expelled the Le from the Hanoi area and were claiming the succession. A regime claiming legitimate succession from the Le was established further south, dominated by the Trinh and the Nguyen. In 1566 Nguyen Hoang obtained an appointment as governor of a southern frontier province. He left the court to take up this command leading a modest but cohesive force of loyal officers and soldiers from his native place in the north on about twenty ships. In 1592 he led his forces north to participate in the expulsion of the Mac usurpers from Thanh Long (modern Hanoi). He returned to the south only in 1600, to counter the rising danger of Mac-related resistance in that quarter.

Mutual suspicion between Trinh and Nguyen already was very high in 1600, but a full break toward the emergence of a separate Nguyen regime came only after Nguyen Hoang's death in 1613. His son came to power in the south largely by hereditary right, surrounded by loyal commanders and troops from the Nguyen native district in the north. His experience of the region's potential, defensible from the north, profitable from maritime trade and expanding agriculture to the south, shaped his attitudes. In effect, one of the aggregations of local power in the hands of a great family and its retainers that for centuries had made the politics of the Red River delta so unstable had been shifted out of the delta into a region where its energies were turned in new directions. The Nguyen had an abundance of naval experience; some of their core forces had come south by sea. Their soldiers were battle-hardened and had considerable experience with firearms.

A thriving cosmopolitan port emerged at Hoi An (the Europeans called it Faifo), not far south of modern Danang. The Nguyen princes did not reside there permanently and kept their control over it relatively low-key; it would remain a sprawling, unkempt Southeast Asian river town with separate quarters for traders from various countries and none of the weight of palace and bureaucracy that shaped Thanh Long. Japanese came in large numbers. Around 1600 they came on the ships of a trade that was licensed and promoted by the Japanese authorities. Later in the century many of them came as exiles, fleeing the persecutions of Christians. Chinese merchants always were numerous and influential, and late in the 1600s there were quite a few who refused to live under the new Qing dynasty, kept the dress and hair of the old Ming dynasty, and were called in Vietnamese "those who burn incense for the Ming."

After Nguyen Hoang died in 1613, his son Nguyen Phuoc Nguyen broke definitively with the Trinh regime in the north, ceasing his fiscal contribution to it in 1620. There were six major military clashes between the two realms between 1627 and 1673. Thereafter both sides were exhausted, and the Trinh were forced to leave the Nguyen in peace. Military office and organization were central to the Nguyen state, and draft for military service the most important and onerous burden on the common people. Imported goods, especially copper for bronze cannon, lead for shot, and saltpeter for gunpowder, were vital to this nation at arms. By about 1615 there was a regular schedule of tolls levied on ships from various countries. Contemporary observers did not think them very high, but the Nguyen realm would not have survived these decades of war without maritime trade revenues, the prosperity brought by maritime trade, and the strategic goods imported.

Japan and England built their new forms of power on a sense of unity that makes their modern nationalism not very surprising. But in these countries and even more in Holland, this sense of unity was compatible with very strong senses of local identity. Nor, as we can see from these Southeast Asian cases and especially from Ayutthaya with its powerful Chinese merchants and even Iranian Muslims, was ethnic, linguistic, and religious diversity an insuperable barrier to the successful development of new forms of profit and power.

For Europeans in 1450 or 1500, the greatest example of how profit and power, trade and armed might reinforced each other was Venice, the great city-state at the head of the Adriatic. Since the 1100s Venice and Genoa, on the west side of the Italian peninsula, had fought many wars for dominance of the Mediterranean, and had even sent convoys of galleys out into the Atlantic and up to the rich ports of what is now Belgium. By 1500 Venice was the dominant power. It sometimes had traded peacefully with the Ottomans, but after 1453 more often was at the head of the shaky Christian alliances opposing them. Its magnificent churches and palaces showed the heritages of the Byzantine Empire and of the world of Islam as well as of Western Europe. Venice was strongly Catholic but frequently in conflict with the popes. Its great Arsenal, the biggest concentration of production in Europe, had more than ten thousand workmen and could turn out a full-sized war galley in a day. It ruled the major ports of the Adriatic, the Peloponnesian Peninsula of Greece, and the islands of Crete and Cyprus, and had major trading interests in every port around the Mediterranean.

Venice was a republic with a sovereign elected for life, the doge. About two thousand men had the right, by inheritance in a particular family line, to participate in the Greater Council. They were eligible for appointment to offices ranging from police functions in the city to generals, ambassadors, and governors of colonial outposts. They elected about two hundred members of a senate, which met every Sunday afternoon to decide on questions of foreign policy, war and peace, and government expenditures. They elected members of higher councils and the doge by very complex voting procedures. The doge, usually elected at the age of sixty or more after a lifetime of service to the republic, was surrounded by ceremony and mystique but was definitely the servant of the collective will of the councils.

It was understood that all the great families represented in these bodies were actively involved in trade, and that the republic lived and died by the profits of trade. In the early 1500s it saw the trade in spices through the ports of the eastern Mediterranean threatened by the Portuguese efforts to control the trade of the Indian Ocean; however the Portuguese blockade eventually proved to be quite porous. Venice led an alliance of Christian fleets in a great victory over the Ottomans at the battle of Lepanto in 1571, but the Ottomans rebuilt their fleets. Venice withdrew from Cyprus and lost Crete to the Ottomans in the 1660s. The republic was no match for the bigger profit-power structures of Britain, the Netherlands, and France.

France in 1690 was a great power in Europe, a feared enemy, known for the size and discipline of its armies and the intelligence and ruthlessness of its diplomacy. Its king, Louis XIV, was the great example of royal wealth and power. Europe today, from Lisbon to St. Petersburg, is dotted with the palaces other kings built in imitation of Louis's Versailles outside Paris, where he kept tight control over his nobility and administered a centralized state. But there are striking differences from the other cases of European profit and power such as England, Holland, and Venice. France had no representative assembly. Local councils were strictly under the control of officials appointed by the king. Merchants could hope to gain great wealth through overseas trading monopolies and provision of fine goods to Versailles, but they found the monarchical state an awkward, interfering patron and did not rush to invest in some of these efforts. In 1685 Louis XIV undercut the commercial prosperity of his own kingdom when he revoked the Edict of Nantes, which had granted very limited toleration to Protestants, driving France's Protestants, including its best merchants, into exile. The French Protestants became conspicuous contributors to the commercial wealth of England, the Netherlands, and rising Prussia, all enemies of France.

France had been a great power in Europe since before 1450. Its central position and its rich agriculture were its basic assets. That wealth supported a large and proud feudal nobility and big cities. The efforts of French kings to centralize governing power and to extend it over outlying regions only loosely subordinate to the monarchy began in the late 1400s. A new use for royal power emerged in the 1490s with invasions and diplomatic maneuvers in Italy, always in opposition to the power of the Austrian-Spanish House of Hapsburg. Francis I, contemporary and occasional rival in royal splendor of Henry VIII of England, pushed centralization as far as he could, but was so short of money that he made great use of the sale of offices to the highest bidders. Unlike Henry, he did not have to deal with a parliament with firm rights to be heard; the French had a tradition of assembly in an Estates General, but it was rarely called and never by Francis.

By the end of Francis's reign in 1547, conflicts between Catholics and Protestants in France were violent and dangerous. Some great nobles became Protestant out of conviction or for political reasons. In the 1560s there was a weak monarchy with young kings, and there were violent conflicts among three great branches of the royal house, one Catholic, one Protestant, one split. The Estates General met but could find no way toward reconciliation. The noble houses led their troops in open battles; some count as many as eight episodes of civil war. On Saint Bartholomew's Day in 1572, mobs in Paris, encouraged by the authorities, killed every Protestant they could find. When a Protestant, Henry IV, came to the throne in 1588, he converted to Catholicism and tried to find a way to give the two sides space to live with each other, but he was assassinated in 1610.

A weak monarchy in a very dangerous military situation was saved from disaster by the diplomatic and administrative skills of the great Cardinal Richelieu. He worked hard to reduce the legal privileges of the Protestants in France, but did not hesitate to ally with foreign Protestant rulers against the power of the Hapsburg Holy Roman Emperors. He destroyed most of the castles that had been the bases of French noble power and put more tax collection in the hands of appointees of the king. His portraits, magnificent in his cardinal's crimson silk robes, show a proud statesman at a rich court, not at all a humble minister of the gospel.

A last round of frightening turmoil and noble rebellion came between 1648 and 1653. In 1651 a mob broke into the Louvre palace in Paris and demanded to see the boy king, Louis XIV; his mother had to agree, and he pretended to be asleep until she managed to get them out. Louis grew up hating Paris and disorder. He built Versailles and other smaller palaces outside Paris and rarely set foot in the Louvre. When his first minister died in 1661, he immediately announced his intention to be his own first minister, to make all final decisions himself. Soon he was reminding his ministers that he was the state. Even earlier French kings had sometimes used the metaphor of the gleaming, life-giving sun—not the sun at the center of the cosmos, which was not yet orthodox opinion—as a metaphor for the monarchy.

Louis made constant and emphatic use of the symbol, cutting a splendid figure when he danced the role of the sun or of Apollo, the sun god, in a court ballet. All Louis's life, the formalities and apparent gaieties of court life concealed hours of document-reading and council meetings by the king and his high ministers. By 1664 he had the ideal detail-oriented, control-minded minister to assist him, Jean-Baptiste Colbert. By prodigious effort Colbert and his modest staff of clerks and provincial appointees uncovered many unauthorized claims of nobility and other cases of fraudulent tax exemption, eliminated many useless offices and other claims on the royal treasury, reduced the indebtedness that weighed so heavily on the royal budget, and increased the efficiency and honesty of tax collection. By 1671 net royal incomes had at least doubled.

After decades of civil war and urban violence, similar impulses to order, hierarchy, and centralization could be seen in many spheres. Paris and other cities were brought under more effective control, the law courts and provincial assemblies had their powers reduced, and controls on publication were elaborated. The nobles found that they had fewer chances to build counter-forces in the provinces. If they wanted access to the many lucrative offices now directly at the king's disposal, and if they wanted their sons to earn their spurs in the king's growing armies, they had to forsake their power bases in the provinces and spend most of their time at the royal court. Louis used his increased tax revenues to expand his kingdom along its fringes and to attempt to dominate its larger neighbors, invading the Netherlands in 1672 and the German lands along the Rhine in 1688.

The revocation of the Edict of Nantes in 1685, ending all legal toleration of Protestants in France, sharpened the sense of the Protestant peoples of England and the Netherlands, who were under one ruler after the successful invasion of England by William III in 1688, that France must be opposed everywhere. The result was a strategic and military confrontation between France and England that continued off and on until the defeat of Napoleon in 1815. The French monarchy was firmly centralized, but, despite Colbert's efforts, its tax structure was inefficient and riddled with exemptions, especially for the nobility. The Estates General still did not meet. The French unification from above, by the imposition of policies and ministers decided by the king and his close ministers, was apparently impressive in the late 1600s. But its intolerance of religious and cultural diversity, and its lack of consultative bodies like the English parliament, the Dutch estates general, and the councils of Venice, made it rigid. That rigidity shattered in world-shaping revolution in 1789.

CHAPTER 5

Settlers and Diasporas, 1610–1640

In the world of the 1500s and 1600s, most people never traveled more than 10 miles from home, or if they did they followed a set of completely familiar migration or trade routes from season to season. So people who did move, voluntarily or against their wills, to strange and distant places, often towns beside a distant sea, shaped the world in important ways.

In 1650 Jamestown in what is now Virginia was the home of a variety of people from England, Scotland, and Ireland, some of whom had come with some money to try to find a new way to get rich; the growing of tobacco was very promising. Others had signed "indentures," paying their ship passage and obliging them to serve a master, often for seven years. When they completed their indentures, some of them would try farming or a skilled craft, and a few would move inland, trade with the Native Americans and perhaps marry one. In 1650 Jamestown was just beginning to have substantial numbers of very different sojourners, slaves from sub-Sahara Africa. It cost a big farmer more to buy a slave than to buy the contract of an indentured servant, but the slave belonged to his or her master until death or sale.

Halfway around the world, the port city of Melaka on the Malay Peninsula had a very different collection of sojourners from afar. It had been ruled by Malay Muslims in the 1400s, by the Portuguese in the 1500s, and after 1641 was under the Dutch East India Company. But a great deal of Melakan trade remained in the hands of people from elsewhere in Asia—Muslims from India, Iran, and the Arabian Peninsula, South Indian Hindus, a few Armenians, and a great many Chinese. Trading diasporas managed most of the trade of many ports around the Indian Ocean and the South China Sea, including Ayutthaya, Hoi An, Manila, and Batavia.

"Diaspora" is a Greek word, meaning "dispersion," first used for the Jews living scattered in the Greek-speaking cities of the eastern Mediterranean after the Roman occupation of Jerusalem and destruction of the Jewish temple in 70 CE. It has come to refer to any dispersion of people whose homeland is occupied by alien conquerors or to which a group cannot return because of persecution. For the slaves of the African diaspora, there was a homeland, but they were completely cut off from it and could not expect any help from it. The Chinese diaspora had a powerful homeland, but one whose rulers generally were indifferent or hostile to Chinese who settled abroad. There may have been times in earlier centuries when Hindu rulers sent fleets into Southeast Asia, but not after 1000 CE. The Armenians had no power-center of their own supporting them. There were a few coherent networks of Muslim diaspora, especially the Hadramis who claimed descent from Muhammad and were influential all around the Indian Ocean. And of course Islam has excellent means of maintaining its integrity wherever it goes, reaffirming its relation to its geographical core every time a Muslim turns toward Mecca in prayer. The pilgrimage to Mecca is a moment of reconnection to the heartland for many people who otherwise are part of a diaspora.

A settler society, by contrast, had continuous backing from the home country and maintained a political connection with it for a long time, as the English did at Jamestown. Its people, settling where local populations were thin or weak (or weakened and thinned by the new diseases of the Columbian Exchange), could set out to recreate in the new place all the society and much of the economy of the homeland. The Spanish and Portuguese societies of the Americas were settler societies in many ways but also were and are today profoundly shaped by the heritages of the indigenous peoples. Throughout the Americas, native people have moved and mixed voluntarily and involuntarily to trade with, work for, or flee the Europeans, producing diasporas of their own.

The stories of diasporas often tell of much hardship as well as of prosperity and social cohesion achieved against great odds. From 1450 to 1700 the Armenian homeland was not a promising center for the exercise of the Armenians' integrity and their many skills. Centered around Mount Ararat in stony plains to the south of the great Caucasus Mountains, it was well placed to dominate trade routes across inner Asia that came around the south end of the Caspian Sea and then branched either along the north shore of the Black Sea or southwest to the Mediterranean. Armenian power and settlement at their height had reached along the latter route down into Cilicia, near the Mediterranean, at the bend where today Syria meets Turkey. In the 1400s the Armenians were very important traders along the north side of the Black Sea, and records can be found of their presence in major trading centers all across Eurasia, from Beijing to Bruges in modern Belgium.

Around 1500 the north side of the Black Sea was under Ottoman rule, and the real opportunities for enterprise were in Istanbul. The Armenian core east of the Black Sea was a battleground between the Ottomans and the Safavids. In 1506 the Safavids occupied part of that core and forcibly transferred most of its Armenian population to areas more firmly under Safavid control. The peasants were settled in Gilan province south of the Caspian, where they contributed to its rise as a major center of silk production. The merchants were settled on the outskirts of Isfahan.

Rarely in world history has a forced relocation opened up such opportunities for the forcibly moved. The great Shah Abbas (reigned 1588–1629) already was making astute use of Georgians and Armenians who had converted to Islam in building up an effective central bureaucracy. The new forced settlers were not required to convert, and they soon took on key roles in the management of main lines of trade, especially the silk trade, where the rural Armenians of Gilan were among the key producers. At New Julfa on the outskirts of Isfahan, they had churches, the headquarters of great merchant houses, and schools that taught their own heritage as one of the first peoples to convert to Christianity and a great deal of sophisticated bookkeeping and commercial management. The great Armenian merchant houses were very helpful to the Safavid shahs in managing key lines of trade and collecting taxes. Other Armenians made themselves very useful and prosperous in close association with the Ottoman rulers at Istanbul. Merchants connected to the great houses spread out on the trade routes from Lisbon to Macao and Manila, trading partly for the home house and partly for themselves, sending detailed reports to the home house, completely trusted.

The Iranian connection did not remain as comfortable for the Armenians after the death of Abbas, but it gave them opportunities to break out into wider trade in two directions. To the north, Armenian silk merchants met Hindus and Muslims from the Mughal realms and Russian traders coming down the Volga at Astrakhan, where the Volga flows into the Caspian Sea. A few adventurous participants in England's trade with Russia made it all the way to Astrakhan and bought Iranian silk there. To the south and east, the Armenians built up a network of trade communities all across India, providing cheap, safe financial transfer services to their own people and others. They had an outpost at Lhasa in Tibet, and some of them joined the annual caravan across the high desert of northern Tibet to Xining in China, where they exchanged silver for gold, which was worth more in India than in China. They were important figures in the trade between the eastern Mediterranean and Ethiopia, where they were welcomed as Christians who knew how to live as islands in a Muslim sea. We even have a record of an Armenian working for the English at the mouth of the Gambia River in West Africa and dying there.

Natives of powerful European kingdoms could also make a diaspora, if they went into exile because they would not follow the required religion. A Huguenot (French Protestant) diaspora spread within Europe when French exiles became important merchants and bankers in Geneva, London, Amsterdam, and Berlin. Late in the 1680s a few hundred French Protestants, refugees from the persecutions of Louis XIV, came to settle under the authority of the Dutch East India Company at the Cape of Good Hope, where they provided sustenance for company ships going to and from Southeast Asia. To go all the way to the little Dutch settlement on the southern tip of Africa was a risky business, but they had been offered generous support and grants of land. The voyage took at least two months and sometimes four or more, with a long stretch around the Equator when the ship was in danger of being becalmed and going nowhere in the stifling heat.

European settlement at the cape extended just a few miles from the little company fort. Drunkenness and prostitution were widespread. The company had no trouble finding people among its former employees who wanted to run a tavern at the cape. The local indigenous people, who called themselves Khoikhoi and whom the Europeans called Hottentots, were glad to sell the company cattle from their herds. But the passing ships also needed supplies of fresh fruit and vegetables. That was why Huguenot farmers were so welcome. Exiled from France, they found the support of a powerful state and company that shared their Protestant faith. Soon many of them settled on the edge of the European settlement zone, in a beautiful valley that they saw would be very good for growing grapes and making wine. There are old French names—Malan, Marais, Du Toit—among the Afrikaner population that ruled South Africa until 1990.

The Huguenots could have stayed peacefully in France if they had been willing to turn Catholic. The settlers of Massachusetts called Pilgrims and Puritans could have stayed quietly in England if they had been willing to be dutiful members of the Church of England. The Quakers who settled Pennsylvania, also often persecuted in England, contributed to the religious variety and moral intensity of American life. And the Catholics who were early settlers of Maryland also were fleeing persecution in England. But none of this could have happened without forms of organization that made possible the settlers' ocean voyages and years of steady supply of an infant colony. Investors in a settlement might be supporting it for religious reasons, but it would be fine if the colony began to produce a profitable export.

The first successful English settlement in mainland North America was at Jamestown. It almost failed several times in its first years; at one point the remaining settlers were on a ship departing for England when a ship with supplies and new settlers appeared on the horizon, and they all went back and started again. Jamestown has gotten bad press in American myth-making, portrayed as full of feckless aristocrats fighting with each other and hunting for gold instead of settling down to farming as the virtuous Pilgrims did just a few years later. This is not entirely wrong, but more recent archeology at the Jamestown site and related scientific studies have shown that it is much too simple. First steps in trading with the nearest Native American people were cordial and promising. Good relations with the Native Americans were essential for a steady food supply; without it the settlers would have been entirely dependent on shipments from the West Indies while they cleared the land for their first crops. But the settlers arrived in 1607, right at the beginning of the worst ten years of drought that can be detected in tree rings from the area. Within about two years the Native Americans told the newcomers they did not even have enough corn to feed their own people. By 1617 the English colonists were passing laws to limit and control relations with the Native Americans, and in 1622 they survived a major attack and retaliated sharply.

The Jamestown venture came at the end of decades of excited discussion in person and in print of how England, a marginal player in the Europe of the late 1500s, could take its place among the European peoples who were profiting from oceanic connections. Reports of Spanish treasure and cruelty, of the spices and other riches of the Indian Ocean, and of the possibilities of quicker routes to Asian waters northwest around the American continent or northeast around Russia, especially those expertly edited, compiled, and sometimes translated by Richard Hakluyt, sold well in Shakespeare's London. The affairs of the tiny colony were supervised by a London-based company, in which Hakluyt, who never traveled farther than Paris, was active. The company failed as early as 1624, but by then it had performed crucial services in sending supplies, publicizing opportunities, selling land grants, and marketing the cash crop that was the key to the success of the venture, tobacco.

Tobacco and smoking were of Native American origin, and the speed with which they spread around the world after the opening of the

Columbian Exchange makes discouraging reading for anyone fighting this public health plague today. It was grown on middle-sized farms close to docks for transportation to England. Expertise in growing and curing grew steadily. The heavy work was done by Englishmen who came as indentured servants and, in later decades, by slaves brought from Africa. The owners, tough pioneers and later some well-funded upper-class refugees from England's civil war, had a share in local government through their representatives in a local assembly that shared power with a governor who was appointed by the Virginia Company and after 1624 by the king. A cash crop, a trade connection, and a representative assembly were enough to allow Virginia to survive and to make some decisions on its own.

Farther north, English settlement took a different form. The core of the group who became the Pilgrims and settled in 1621 at Plymouth in what now is Massachusetts were from a village named Scrooby in northern England. They were mostly people of meager status and education. They were "Separatists," that is, they insisted on the autonomous organization of every Christian congregation, and refused all connection with the Church of England. Deciding that they could not wait for the long struggle to purify the Church of England but wanted to establish a true Biblical society without delay, they endured harsh prison sentences in England and explored various projects to settle in America before they left England and tried life in the Netherlands in 1608. There, like some evangelical Christians trying to raise children in Los Angeles or Amsterdam in our own times, they worried about their children speaking a foreign language and growing up in a society where everything seemed to be permitted.

Despite their lack of power and social standing, the Separatists had connections with influential people in London who were willing to help them arrange a move to the New World. Other influential people seem to have thought that it would make sense to get the Separatists out of the way if it could be done without causing trouble for any other budding colony, and that there might be money to be made in trading with the Native Americans for furs and in fishing.

A confusing variety of investment schemes and "patents" for settlement in one area or another came and went; when about a hundred people sailed from Plymouth in southern England on the Mayflower in 1621, another plan was still awaiting the king's approval. Preparing to land and build their first houses, the migrants entered into a "compact" to govern themselves, in form only a temporary arrangement until it could be approved or other arrangements made in London.

Negotiations continued, and there were some near misses in getting full legalization, but in fact the successful self-government of Plymouth, like the representative assembly in Virginia, was simply a result of London's acceptance of what worked and its inability to control events so far across the sea. The Plymouth settlers spread out on small farms, took up fishing, and traded with the natives. Trade for furs farther north, on the coast of modern Maine, was especially successful. After 1630 Plymouth was somewhat in the shadow of the larger Puritan enterprise in the Boston area, but it maintained its autonomy and vitality throughout the 1600s.

The Puritans who settled around what now is Boston were much more influential and better connected in England than the Pilgrims had been, with ties to several important London lawyers and even the earl of Lincoln. Their financing and organization were excellent; they sent one thousand people to Massachusetts in their first year, 1630. By 1642 sixteen thousand migrants had arrived in Massachusetts—not a large number in world-historical terms, but enough to make a settled society and to expand into new lands. They also managed a much more formal move toward colonial self-government, writing the charter of the Massachusetts Bay Company in such a way that the settlers were leading voting participants in the company, took the charter document with them to Massachusetts, and dodged demands that it be returned to England.

The Civil War of the 1640s left king and parliament with no time for such distant matters. But it is hard to see how the Massachusetts company's self-government was in fact more secure than that of Virginia or Plymouth, and in all three cases the distractions of the 1640s and 1650s in England contributed greatly to a buildup of experience and precedent in self-government. In Massachusetts this was very much the self-government of the godly minority; only full members of the church were voting freemen, and no one could become a church member without being convinced, and convincing the exacting church elders, that he had really received God's saving grace. Other areas of New England were settled in later decades by frontiersmen trading with the Native Americans along the Connecticut River and Long Island Sound; by Puritans even narrower in belief and practice than those in Massachusetts, at New Haven (now in Connecticut); and by refugees from Puritan conformity who were among the first to proclaim a complete separation of religion and governing, in what is now Rhode Island.

The story of the European settlement of Virginia and Massachusetts often has been told as if there was a line, a frontier, that moved west as Europeans advanced and Native Americans retreated, succumbed to epidemics, and sometimes fought back. But there never was a line. There was a wide and long-lasting zone, a "middle ground," in which neither side was completely in charge, and newcomers and Natives interacted and sometimes managed to get along. In Massachusetts we can see it before the landing at Plymouth, as Native Americans traded with transient fishermen and explorers and were especially eager to obtain metal goods—knives, axe heads, cooking pots. Sometimes they sold the visitors food, but the great commodity they could supply to the European market was beaver skins. The fine, water-repellent undercoat of these pelts could be made into a glossy waterproof felt, which was the preferred material for European men's hats from the 1500s to the 1800s.

The expansion of the middle ground continued as some settlers ventured far beyond their villages and farms, living, marrying, and trading in Native American society, while some Native Americans converted and settled in villages of "Praying Indians." The middle ground was especially important to the north and south of Massachusetts, where the Saint Lawrence and Hudson rivers opened the way to the rich heart of the continent, so that by 1650 or 1700 a zone of trade and ethnic and cultural mixing reached to the Great Lakes and the Mississippi River.

The Dutch established trading posts on the Hudson River, on Manhattan Island, and at modern Albany from 1624 to 1626. Well placed to tap the inland fur trade networks, the colony made only halting progress. Until 1640 few settlers could be found, because the Netherlands was prosperous and tolerant and the West India Company, monopolistic rulers of the colony, would not allow individual settlers to participate in the fur trade. In the 1640s expansion of Dutch trade and settlement provoked major counter-attacks by some of the most prosperous and best-organized Native Americans north of Mexico, the Iroquois, and those almost drove the Dutch out.

Thereafter the Dutch dealt warily with the Iroquois to keep their access to the fur trade. Nearer to Nieuw Amsterdam relations with the Algonkian and Delaware people worsened as more Dutch settlers arrived. Many of them moved out to start small farms. They put fences around their cultivated fields and let their pigs and cattle roam free in the forests, where they ruined some of the cultivated fields, not surrounded by fences, of the Native Americans. The authorities in Nieuw Amsterdam did nothing to answer Native American complaints. Occasional Native American attacks led to an attack by well-armed Dutch soldiers on a Native American village in 1641, in which more than two hundred Native Americans were hacked to death or burned alive in their own houses. A nasty guerrilla war dragged on until 1645, completely destroying the local trade in furs and in food supplies for Nieuw Amsterdam. Year by year the Dutch were pushed out of the Connecticut River valley by the more numerous English. When a squadron of English warships trained its guns on the Nieuw Amsterdam fort in 1665, the Dutch surrendered without firing a shot, and Nieuw Amsterdam became New York.

The Dutch presence on the Hudson set off enormous changes for the Native American peoples south of Lake Ontario, five groups with a common language and culture we call the "five nations" of the Iroquois. Trade goods and disease came to them together after the Dutch settled at Albany in 1624. By the 1640s the Iroquois had lost half their population. It was their custom to deal with loss of a male relative by going to war and capturing a male from another people, who would be forcibly adopted into the community or sometimes tortured to death. The great losses of population, and the constant need for trade goods, now including guns, powder, and shot, propelled the Iroquois into fierce attacks on their neighbors in all directions, including the Dutch along the Hudson and the Native Americans trading with the French along the Saint Lawrence River. Native American refugees from these wars spread out into the middle of the continent, so that the middle ground of the traders also was a mixing ground of Native American cultures.

By the 1660s the Iroquois were fighting among themselves and faced growing English and French military forces. For many generations they had kept peace among themselves by periodic meetings of their leaders, always with mourning ceremonies for those who had died and many speeches. Now they adapted these ceremonies to make peace among themselves and with the French and the British. Leaders arriving for such a meeting were greeted with an exchange of gifts and of condolences for dead relatives and a ceremony of wiping tears from the eyes, unplugging the ears, and cleansing the throats of those who had made a long journey. The re-affirmation of personal connection was all-important. In one French description, a Mohawk "took hold of a Frenchman, placed his arm within his, and with his other arm he clasped that of an Algonquin.... 'Here,' he said, 'is the knot that binds us inseparably.... Even if the lightning were to fall upon us, it could not separate us; for if it cuts off the arm that holds you to us, we will at once seize each other by the [other] arm.' And thereupon he turned around, and caught the Frenchman and the Algonquin by their two arms—holding them so closely that he seemed unwilling ever to leave them."[1]

The governors of the English colonies seem to have thought that by their participation in such meetings they were building a system of binding commitments to English sovereignty over the Native American peoples; for the Iroquois participants, the affirmation of a face-to-face relation, even with a former enemy, was the main point of the ceremony. In the noble words of an Iroquois chief, "Be not dissatisfied; should we not embrace this happiness offered to us, that is, peace, in the place of war? Yea, we shall take the evil-doers, the Senecas by the hand, and La Barre [a French commander] likewise, and their ax and their sword shall be thrown into a deep water."[2]

The Saint Lawrence was navigable all the way to modern Montreal for seagoing ships. Around 1500 Portuguese, Spanish, and French fishermen came in great numbers to catch cod and sometimes to dry them in temporary shore settlements on the coast of Newfoundland. Soon whalers joined the fishermen. There were no permanent European settlements, but Native Americans quickly learned that they could trade their furs for metal knives and pots. In 1534, a French exploratory voyage under Jacques Cartier described an encounter with Native Americans: "The next day some of these Indians came in nine canoes.... As soon as they saw us they began to run away, making signs that they had come to barter with us; and held up some furs of small value.... We...sent two men on shore, to offer them some knives and other iron goods, and a red cap to give to their chief. Seeing this they sent on shore part of their people with some of their furs; and the two parties traded together." In the 1590s an English captain reported that the local people were becoming middlemen, using European whaling boats, "wearing various items of European clothing...speaking a half-Basque, half-Indian trade jargon."[3]

The French settlement at what is now Quebec City was founded in 1608. Along the Saint Lawrence, only a narrow strip was suitable for European-style agriculture. Land was held, as in France, by quasi-noble *seigneurs* (landlords), who leased it to farmers, owned the gristmills, and thoroughly dominated the local scene. In the few towns there were many soldiers and officials and no representative assemblies. The Roman Catholic Church was a major presence, the seigneurial landlord of one-third of the colony's farmers. Its missionary efforts among the natives produced some excellent, observant writing by the missionaries, some impressively devoted converts, and quite a lot of conflict within kinship groups when some converted and others did not.

The Saint Lawrence was above all a superb opening into the interior of the continent. Once the French had learned about birchbark canoes

BALAENA ERECTA GRANDEM NAVEM SVBMERGENS.

Videntur & alia quædam cete ex eodem Balænis adnumeranda, quæ ipſe ſimpliciter cete no
minat, cum præter magnitudinem balænis præcipuè conuenientem, nullam in ſe corporis par-
tem raram aut monſtroſam habeant. Eiuſmodi ſunt:

CETVS INGENS, QVEM INCOLAE FARAE INSVLAE ICH-
thyophagi tempeſtatibus appulſum, unco comprehenſum ferreo, ſecu-
ribus diſſecant & partiuntur inter ſe.

NAVTAE IN DORSA CETORVM, QVAE INSVLAS PVTANT,
anchoras figentes ſæpe periclitantur. Hos ceros Trolual ſua lingua
appellant, Germanicè Teiffelwal.

*Men at sea feared monstrous
whales rising from the deep.
The hunting of whales for
the oil extracted from their
blubber led Europeans to many
new oceans and coasts. In a
German book from the 1550s,
an image of the stripping of the
blubber from a whale carcass
is framed by nightmare scenes
of a whale attacking a ship and
sailors on the back of a whale
that they have mistaken for an
island. Library of Congress,
LC-USZ62-95207.*

from the natives, the way was open from the Montreal area up the
Ottawa River and via easy portages to Lake Nipissing, on to the Great
Lakes, and by more easy portages from Lake Michigan into the Mississippi River system. Beaver and hospitable natives seemed to be everywhere. The Frenchmen who learned from the natives and lived among
them became *coureurs de bois*, "runners of the woods," masters of
adaptation to the middle ground. By 1611 they were on Lake Michigan,
by 1660 on Lake Superior, by 1673 on the Mississippi River, and in a
final amazing extension of the contact zone two of them, badly treated
by the French authorities, defected in the 1660s and guided the English

into Hudson's Bay and a whole new world of fur-trading in what is now western Canada.

Wealth, influence, and religious dissent came together in distinctive forms in the founding of Maryland and Pennsylvania. George Calvert, Lord Baltimore, announced his conversion to Roman Catholicism in 1619, at a time of rising anti-Catholic feeling and policy. His excellent connections at the English court and among the promoters of Virginia led to a very generous grant of proprietorship in Maryland in 1632. The first colonists reached Chesapeake Bay early in 1634. Maryland was the only place formally under British rule where Roman Catholics could worship openly. By 1650 the colony had substantial numbers of Protestant settlers as well as Catholics and confronted the hostility of the Puritan government in London, but Lord Baltimore and the Maryland assembly declared freedom of conscience and worship for all Christians.

Pennsylvania also was the creation of a very well-placed religious outsider and an English government that was not averse to sending troublemakers off to distant colonies. William Penn was the son of the lord admiral of England, a key supporter of the restoration of the monarchy in 1660. He also was a Quaker, a member of the Society of Friends, one of the most radically pacifist and anti-hierarchical movements in English Christianity. A few Quakers had begun to settle along the Delaware River in 1675, and William Penn was inspired to seek a grant of land in America where the Quakers could take refuge. King Charles II and his brother James, the Duke of York, liked the idea; they could justify it to a degree as compensation for salary never paid to the admiral and show their broad-mindedness and generosity to troublesome subjects. And if the colony succeeded, some of those subjects would be settled a long way indeed from London. Their generosity was staggering; the colony had an area of 45,000 square miles. Penn could not even object to their decision to name it Pennsylvania, since it was done ostensibly in honor of the late admiral. The charter did not give Penn powers quite as absolute as Lord Baltimore had in Maryland to the south, but still he could shape things pretty much as he wished.

Penn soon was talking of his colony as his "Holy Experiment," where Quaker principles could be put into practice. It comes as no surprise to find such a marvelous combination—the heritage of holiness and the openness to experiment—inspired by the piety and the radical individualism of the Quaker way. The Frame of Government that ultimately was adopted allowed many settlers to vote for members of an assembly, which shared power with a smaller council. Penn himself sailed for Pennsylvania in 1682. He found his little colony thriving and was delighted by the climate and the abundance of nature. The Delaware native people, with whom he strove to deal on terms of friendship and equity, especially impressed him. "For their persons, they are generally tall, straight, well built, and of singular proportion; they tread strong and clever, and mostly walk with a lofty chin.... Their language is lofty, yet narrow, but like the Hebrew.... But in liberality they excel; nothing is too good for their friend. Give them a fine gun, coat, or other thing, it may pass twenty hands before it sticks; light of heart, strong affections, but soon spent....they never have much, nor want much."[4] He also described the oratory and procedures of their councils. Trying to fit them into the biblical story of mankind, he suspected that they were descended from the Ten Lost Tribes of Israel.

The peoples of all diasporas longed for the homeland and regretted leaving it. But most had done so to some degree voluntarily; all the Pilgrim fathers would have had to do was become good members of the Church of England, and they could have lived out their lives comfortably in England. Not so the exiled Africans. A typical experience of an African brought to Brazil, for example, involved a capture in war or raid somewhere in the interior of what is now Angola, a long, forced march to the coast, and a horrified first sight of the big ships and of the big cauldrons on the beach, used to prepare food for the slaves, but which some thought were used to cook the slaves themselves. Then followed the long misery of the "middle passage," locked below decks most of the time on a pitching ship, infections spreading rapidly among people packed together, seasick and suffering from intestinal ailments. In the port the slave was auctioned to a planter, and then usually would have years, usually just a few before the release of death, of exhausting labor on a sugar plantation.

There have been many varieties of slavery and bondage. In traditional African societies quite a few people were in some form of bondage. But none of them was quite like the "chattel slavery" of Africans in the New World, in which the slave was purely and simply property and had no standing as a human being. People in bondage in African societies were not free to leave their villages or their social roles, and their positions in society were lowly ones, but they were dealt with as human beings with human connections. Their children might have less lowly positions. Slaves might occupy positions of considerable prestige and responsibility, in the household or army of a king.

Control over people was the most important form of wealth and power in Africa, where control of a piece of land meant nothing, since the land lost its fertility after being farmed for a few years. A big man was not a big landholder but one with many dependents. Those dependents might be children of dependents, war captives, or people convicted of violations of customary law. Not many of them could be sold to another chief or village. There was some trading of slaves, even over long distances; as the Portuguese groped down the west coast of Africa, they tapped an already existing northward trade in slaves as well as gold and ivory.

Portuguese traders bought slaves in African ports, and they brought some of them to Spanish and Portuguese settlements in the Americas. Soon, first on the West African island of São Tomé and then in Brazil, the Portuguese began to employ them on sugar plantations, where at harvest season cutting cane and boiling sugar went on around the clock in exhausting heat. This was the economic key to a growing European demand for African slaves, from modest beginnings in the 1500s to the great sugar and slaves boom of the Caribbean in the 1700s. Large sectors of the economies of the Americas became completely dependent on African labor. The descendants of the conquistador Cortés had African slaves working alongside their native laborers in sugar fields before 1550. The Bahia and Pernambuco areas of what is now northeast Brazil were the first great centers of this "plantation complex," one of the great forces of global integration in early modern times, in which cheap forced labor combined with production of a novel consumer good for distant markets.

When the Dutch occupied parts of Brazil in the 1600s and then were driven out, they took that complex to the Caribbean islands, where after 1650 sugar production and slave labor expanded rapidly. African slaves were important bearers of expert knowledge of sugar production from São Tomé to Brazil to Barbados, Hispaniola, Jamaica, and many more islands. Elsewhere in the Americas, Africans were valued for other skills they brought from Africa, including iron-working, mining, diving for pearls, and herding cattle on horseback. Slaves who worked in a town, the men as blacksmiths, carters, and other skilled trades, the women often selling things in the market place, might be allowed to move around and seek work on their own as long as they paid an agreed share to their owners. They might even have some social life and religious association on their own.

The total number of African slaves transported to Europe and the Americas before 1600 was not much more than 200,000. Between 1600 and 1700 there were 1,200,000, including more than 600,000 between 1676 and 1700, of whom about 300,000 went to the rapidly developing sugar islands of the Caribbean. African rulers and traders usually kept control over the trade at the African end. As late as the 1680s, the English bought many of their slaves on the "Windward Coast," roughly the coast of modern Liberia and Cote d'Ivoire, where they had no settled forts or stations but simply kept a lookout from a ship until they saw a smoke signal from African traders who had slaves for sale. Farther east at Whydah, in modern Benin, the local ruler kept a firm hand on the trade and kept all slaves in stockades supervised by his own officials until they were sold, paid for, and taken to the waiting European ships. In Congo, relations that began with correspondence between the kings of Portugal and Congo ended in Portuguese slave-raiders' involvement in a disastrous civil war and a continued massive export of slaves from Luanda.

For the Africans involved in the slave trade, slavery and the buying and selling of human beings were ordinary activities. They knew, at some level, that selling people to be taken away on ships was not the same as selling them to a neighboring people a hundred miles away. They cannot have had a very clear sense of the horrors of the middle passage, or the way slaves were worked to death on the sugar plantations, or the way they were treated simply as property, no different from cattle, not as subordinate human beings. By 1650 or 1700, many African rulers and traders had become accustomed to goods imported in the trade, from rum to felt hats to muskets, and did not want to try to get along without them. Muskets were not necessarily indispensable for African warfare, but a king would not want to risk losing a war because he did not have them and wind up on the middle passage himself.

Captains of slave ships usually preferred to keep their slaves alive; each one was a substantial investment. But some believed that the return was better on a "tight-packed" ship, where more died but more were delivered alive. The slaves were confined below decks most of the time. Many were desperately sick. People said you could smell a slave ship from a long way downwind. For those who survived the voyage, there was an auction, often a further journey by land or sea, and then brutally hard work. For most kinds of work, more men were wanted than women. Even where slave couples formed bonds and had children, they could be torn apart by the sale of one of them. Punishments were arbitrary and brutal. The average life expectancy of a sugar plantation slave was seven years. Young males were especially prized for their physical strength in the fields, young women for their "breeding" potential, so many slaves died before the age of twenty-five or thirty. The slaves on a plantation might be from various parts of Africa, without a common language.

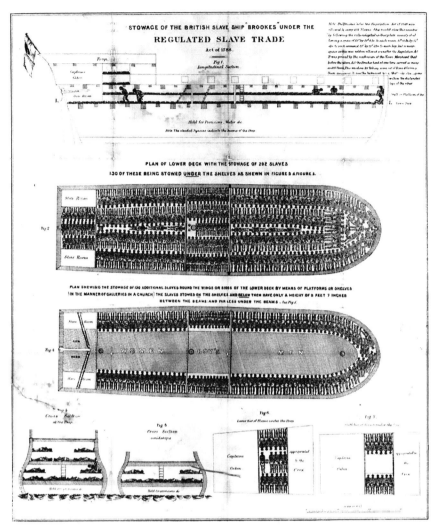

A plan for packing slaves for the voyage across the Atlantic shows a terrifying impulse to efficiency. Some experts advocated tight packing; more slaves would die, but the profits per voyage would be higher. Library of Congress, LC-USZ62-44000.

Amazingly under these terrible conditions, the slaves managed to preserve some pieces of an African heritage and put them together in African-American and especially African-Caribbean and African-Brazilian forms of society, culture, and religion. A ship supplying slaves to a particular island might bring a human cargo of peoples of similar languages and cultures from one or two African ports. A plantation owner often found it cheaper to let his slaves have plots of land to raise their own food than to import all their food. There were plantations where almost all the slaves spoke the same African language and where stable marriage-like relations were common. Observers noted African styles in hair-dressing, clothes, pottery, and music. Slave-owners worried that drums might be signals for revolt but were more tolerant of singing and stringed instruments.

Even if a single African culture and language could not be preserved, not all was lost. In cities from Brazil to Virginia, in rural areas, and in remote refuges where escaped slaves built their own societies, people of African descent shaped the cultures and societies of the New World. Many Africans were products of a coastal trading world in which several languages were spoken, including a European one. Some were exposed to Christianity already in Africa, more in the Americas. The powers of the saints and angels of Roman Catholicism seemed not altogether different from those of the old gods. In Spanish American cities, slaves sometimes organized religious associations that worshipped a Catholic saint with a strong flavor of a particular African ethnic heritage. The use of kinship terms, of parents and children and uncles and aunts, pervasive in West Africa to this day, could be used to re-build human connections torn apart by slavery. The results are still with us, in a rich range of "creole" languages and dialects, in custom and folklore, and in the strongly African folk-religions of Haiti, Cuba, and Brazil.

Slaves did revolt on the ships and the plantations, but before 1700 they always were crushed. A more effective form of resistance was escape and the formation of an African community in the backcountry, sometimes in alliance with the native peoples. Escaped slaves built a community that survived for decades in the convoluted mountain country of Jamaica. At Palmares in the interior of northeast Brazil, escaped slaves built a self-sufficient and well-defended community that survived for more than a hundred years, until 1694. In French, Dutch, and English plantation colonies on the north coast of South America some slaves probably were building communities in the interior by 1700; their descendants, preserving a synthesized African culture, still are found there today. The African diaspora has been a fundamental shaping force in the Americas since before 1600, and it remains so today.

A very different diaspora, voluntary and prosperous, had emerged around the Indian Ocean and the South China Sea by about 1200. Ibn Battuta, an Arab travel writer, tells us that when he lived in Kozhikode on the southwest coast of India in the 1330s, ten or more big Chinese trading ships came there every year. Around 1200 at the latest, Champa, in what is now southern Vietnam, had officials who probably were émigré Chinese but were in no way agents of the Song dynasty that ruled China, in charge of trade and imported luxury goods. Shards of Chinese porcelain from before 1400 are found on beaches and in graves and shipwrecks from the Philippines to the east coast of Africa. The founding king of the Ayutthaya monarchy about 1350 in what is now Thailand is said to have had a Chinese mother. But a coherent picture of the first phase of the Chinese diaspora, about 1100 to 1400, is remarkably elusive. While the Chinese have been the world's best keepers of reliably dated historical records, we have only scraps of Chinese sources about the Chinese diaspora in Southeast Asia before 1400, and we are not that much better off for the sixteenth and seventeenth centuries. Although the Chinese elite and state were not always actively hostile to maritime trade, they rarely promoted it, and people involved in it preferred to keep commercially valuable information in private networks.

The third emperor of the Ming dynasty, who ruled from 1402 to 1424, sent great fleets of ships as far as India, on the tracks of this shadowy first diaspora. These fleets attacked and defeated a Chinese strong man who was dominating the southeast coast of Sumatra and left behind a substantial number of settlers who managed the tribute embassies sent to China by Siam, Melaka, Champa, and probably other coastal states in Southeast Asia. These embassies, following the ceremonies of a lesser ruler presenting tribute to the Chinese "Son of Heaven," were the sole legal channel for maritime trade after the Ming emperors, alarmed by the power of Japanese pirates and their Chinese associates, forbade all maritime trading by China-based ships and people. Thus Chinese who settled in Southeast Asia were well placed to take advantage of the great worldwide expansion of maritime trade in the 1500s. They helped the Portuguese make their first contacts with Siam and China and probably in their conquest of Melaka. They were key players at the open port of Banten on the west end of Java.

Chinese already were trading in the Philippines when the first Spaniards arrived there in 1571. A fleet of Chinese pirates almost wiped out Manila in its first year, but then the Chinese discovered the immense profits of bringing Chinese silks and other goods to Manila and taking American silver back to China. There were far more Chinese than Spaniards at Manila. They set the terms of trade. They dominated all the crafts and trades, including such thoroughly European ones as bread-making and bookbinding. Some of them converted to Catholicism. Many of these conversions must have been for safety and respectability in Spanish eyes, but the Dominican fathers who ministered to the Chinese found some of them to be intelligent and devout. By 1600 the Spanish recognized one Christian

Chinese as "captain" of the community. The Chinese contracted with the Spanish authorities to collect many kinds of taxes on local trade.

When agents of the Ming court who had heard of the riches of Manila visited in 1603, tensions over Spanish tax collections from the Chinese community and by Chinese contractors from the native Filipinos exploded. Some new Chinese arrivals, who had the least to lose, may have begun the violence, but Spanish guns and Filipino numbers soon prevailed, and between 15,000 and 25,000 Chinese were massacred. Almost immediately the Spanish realized that they could not survive without Chinese residents and Chinese trade. The Ming authorities blamed the people who had set up the 1603 visit and did not retaliate against the Spanish. The silk-for-silver trade across the Pacific went on to see some of its best years between 1604 and 1610.

In the 1630s large numbers of Chinese who were hired by Chinese land developers to do the heavy work of opening up rice cultivation around the big lake east of Manila rebelled and were savagely repressed by Spanish troops and Filipino auxiliaries. In 1662 the Chinese maritime leader who had just expelled the Dutch from Taiwan threatened to invade, and there still were rumors of Chinese invasion in the 1680s. But the trade continued, and the local Chinese contracted with the Spanish to collect most of the taxes on trade in the Manila area. In later centuries Chinese entrepreneurs and shopkeepers spread out to many other places in the islands.

The people who made long voyages from China and settled in distant places in the 1500s and 1600s mostly came from one region, the southern coast of Fujian province. The strategies they developed for surviving and prospering in one area were then applied to another. Thus a form of negotiation for sale prices of all of a year's imports from China, developed at Manila, later seems to have been used in Chinese trade at Nagasaki in Japan. At Manila Chinese also served the Spanish as "tax farmers," that is, a private individual or group would contract with the authorities to collect a certain tax, delivering an agreed-on amount to the public treasury and keeping the rest. Comparable practices were widespread in early modern Europe and India, and must have seemed quite ordinary to all concerned. "Tax farming" is attractive to a government that needs revenue and has limited manpower and administrative reach. The risk for the "farmer" is that he will not collect enough and will have to pay part of the contracted amount out of his own funds. The risks for the state are that it will yield part of its power to private parties, or that if the "farmers" are too heavy-handed, people's hatred of them will rub off on the state. The second danger can be minimized by using outsiders as tax farmers: Jews in Europe, Muslims in southern India, Chinese at Manila and elsewhere in Southeast Asia.

When the Dutch East India Company established its great power base at Jakarta on western Java and renamed it Batavia, Chinese settlers from Fujian already were in the area. An extremely astute merchant named Su Minggang was appointed the first "captain" of the Batavia Chinese, and he became an indispensable ally and adviser of the formidable Jan Pieterszoon Coen, second governor-general of the Dutch company, brutal and effective enforcer of monopolies. Tax farming practices quite similar to those at Manila were put in place. Chinese sojourners loved to gamble, and the monopoly on their gambling was "farmed" to wealthy Chinese and was a major source of income to the Dutch. Small taxes on the Chinese community funded construction works on which poor Chinese earned their daily bowl of rice and provided for a Chinese hospital.

When the Dutch established a trading center on the southwest coast of Taiwan in 1624, Chinese merchants based in Japan advised them and brought them Chinese silks and other exports. Su Minggang himself spent some time in Taiwan, organizing the beginnings of sugar cane and rice farming. This shift to farming also was occurring in Java and Luzon. Up to this time, Chinese emigration had been largely in search

In the markets of Batavia, modern Jakarta, people from all around the Indian Ocean jostle around the stalls full of beautiful tropical fruit. The man on the right is Chinese, the women Javanese, the cockatoo perhaps from barely known Australia. Rijksmuseum, Amsterdam.

of commercial opportunity and had focused on royal capitals and other major trade ports. The thousands of Chinese who came to Taiwan and worked in the sugar and rice fields were fleeing from the chaos of the late Ming rebellions and the Qing conquest. They were less at ease with Dutch rule—and the exactions of Chinese tax farmers—than the big merchants; they rebelled against the Dutch in 1652 and were brutally put down. In 1661 many of them welcomed an invasion from the Fujian coast that brought an end to Dutch rule on Taiwan. In 1662 and 1663 the Chinese conquerors of Taiwan threatened to go on to attack Manila. Their leader died, and they did not, but the Spanish had had good reason to fear that the local Chinese would support them.

Another area where Chinese emigrants increasingly went into farming was the Mekong Delta, now southern Vietnam, where large numbers of Chinese fled from the Ming-Qing chaos. Peace on the China coast after 1680 did nothing to slow the flow of emigrants, and it probably increased now that travel was safer. The area around Batavia was the destination of many poor Chinese, who worked in the sugar plantations of established Chinese merchants and nourished grievances against them and the Dutch that would explode in rebellion in 1740.

The study of diasporas cannot neglect the Jews, the people for whom the word diaspora was invented. The most important development in Jewish history between 1450 and 1700 was a new forced diaspora, as the Jewish communities of Spain and Portugal, which had thrived under Muslim rulers, were forced into exile or far underground by the persecutions of the Catholic monarchs beginning in 1492; Jews and Muslims could stay in Spain and Portugal only if they accepted Catholic baptism and discipline. Some of these exiles, called Sephardim (a term that may refer in the Bible to early exiles from Jerusalem but is generally understood to refer to people settled in Spain and Portugal), settled in Amsterdam, where they became major participants in the stock market and maintained a vibrant cultural life with much interchange with Christian artists and intellectuals. The painter Rembrandt lived on the edge of the Jewish district and had many Jewish friends. A member of the community in the 1680s wrote—in Spanish—the first known book on how to make money in the stock market. The philosopher Benedict de Spinoza had non-Jewish admirers, strayed too far from the Jewish tradition, and was expelled from the congregation. In the mid-1600s, the Sephardim built the splendid Portuguese-Jewish Synagogue, which still stands in Amsterdam.

But the great refuge for the Sephardim after 1492 was the Ottoman Empire, especially Istanbul and Salonika. The Jews of Istanbul were a recognized community of the people of the Book. The chief rabbi probably was not as important a figure as the Greek Orthodox patriarch, but he was recognized and consulted. There are still Sephardic congregations in Istanbul today, and they still sing some of their hymns in Ladino, a form of old Spanish adapted to Jewish needs and written in the Hebrew alphabet. There was a Hebrew printing press in Istanbul before 1500.

Jerusalem also was ruled by the Ottomans. Jews could worship at the Western Wall of the Temple Mount, as they do today, but the great Muslim shrines of the Haram al-Sharif occupied the top of the mount. Safed near the Sea of Galilee was a center of Jewish settlement and learning. In the 1660s Sabbatai Sevi, a Jewish mystic from Izmir, in modern Turkey, proclaimed that he was the long-awaited messiah; Jewish leaders condemned his visions and his violations of tradition, but many Jews scattered in the diaspora responded with hope and excitement, and began to make preparations to join him in Jerusalem. The Ottoman authorities saw him as a threat to the multi-ethnic order of their empire and arrested him. He saved his neck and betrayed his followers by converting to Islam.

Settler societies, diaspora communities, creole societies speaking Spanish and Portuguese, far-flung Muslim communities—all faced the common challenge of keeping the old ways, the old faith, the old language, in new and alien worlds. One solution was to found a school. The hiring of a teacher from the Arabic-speaking heartland for a Koranic school was one of the first goals of any new Muslim community. The children learning to read Hebrew, the solitary scholar, and the circle of men around the study table were at the heart of the life of any Jewish community. Christian communities were especially eager to educate their own ministers. The University of Santo Tomas in Manila traces its history to a Dominican seminary founded in 1611. The little Puritan settlement in Massachusetts Bay founded a college for training ministers in 1636, just fifteen years after the first settlers arrived; it was supported by a gift from an English Puritan named John Harvard and formed the tiny beginning of what is today Harvard University.

An even stronger support of continuity and identity was family. When servants and shopkeepers spoke different languages and worshipped different gods, the need to preserve language and custom within the family was especially great. It was one of the sources of an emphasis on marrying within the community that was common to all diasporas and of the great effort many of them made to keep accurate genealogies. This was, of course, hardest in the African diaspora, where slaves on a single plantation often were from many African peoples and where the sale of slaves often tore family units apart, but even here there were successes. For Jews, it was a special moment to see a young couple standing under the wedding canopy, joining and perpetuating the community. And the great annual confirmation of identity and continuity was a family dinner, the Passover seder, with its special food, the children gathered around the table, the questions for them: "Why is this night different from all other nights?" and the final diasporic blessing: "L'shanah haba-ah b'yerushalayim...Next year may we be in Jerusalem."

CHAPTER 6

Time of Troubles, 1640–1670

Between 1630 or 1640 and 1670, several parts of the world that were only loosely interconnected with each other suffered through years of war, rebellion, and plague. In just one decade, 1640–1650, Parisian mobs rampaged through the city and threatened the boy king in his bedroom in the Louvre palace; a revolutionary military government in England executed King Charles I, the executioner holding up the severed head to a huge, silent crowd; and the citizens of Yangzhou, one of China's richest and most sophisticated cities, suffered through ten days of random killing, looting, and burning by Manchu soldiers with their alien language and shaved foreheads. But by 1690 at the latest, France, England, China, and many other areas had entered a new phase of stability and rising prosperity.

The crisis of the seventeenth century has been interpreted as the struggle of a new urban bourgeois order to overthrow the remnants of a feudal order based on power over land and peasants. Some historians thought that a big downturn in silver production in the Spanish Empire caused the money supply to contract, and that might have set off a commercial depression, intensifying the normal struggle for survival. The growth of population, according to another view, made life harder for ordinary people and made competition for elite positions harsher. Some noted that these years seem to have seen a periodic maximum of sunspots, with a pattern of cooler weather and poor harvests. These explanations all have some relevance in explaining many cases of mid-century turmoil. But there was a very different pattern of change in Japan, which was past its cycle of disorder by 1640, and turmoil in the Muslim gunpowder empires had different consequences.

China did not have to struggle to build a centralized state apparatus as did the English, the French, and the Japanese. In fact, when Europeans began to visit China and write about it in the sixteenth century, they found in Chinese government some kinds of effectiveness their rulers in Europe could only dream of. The Chinese emperors did not confront a nobility entrenched in hereditary privilege, nor cities with autonomous

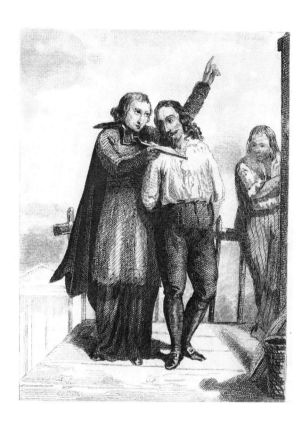

A Church of England clergyman says a last prayer over the condemned King Charles I in 1649. A huge, silent crowd watched as he was beheaded. Library of Congress, LC-USZ62-77770.

rights. They ruled through magistrates who obtained their positions by passing a series of demanding examinations testing their knowledge of Chinese classical texts and their ability to apply their moral lessons to political and administrative problems. Knowing no such career open to talent in the Europe of their day, the early Jesuit missionaries were very much impressed. One of them wrote in amazement, "Only such as have earned a doctor's degree or that of licentiate are admitted to take part in the government of the kingdom."[1] China's rulers came far closer to the ideal of uniform administration reaching out to the boundaries of a unified state than the rulers of any other part of the world except Japan. Chinese craftsmen produced the best textiles and the only porcelain in the world. These goods moved through the empire and into world trade through the hands of skillful, well-organized merchants, earning China a consistent inflow of silver. China was in many ways as close to the emerging "early modern" patterns of administrative unity and economic productivity as any part of the world. But China also suffered through a cycle of violence in the mid-1600s.

All Chinese scholar-officials were the products of long years of studying Chinese history and classical texts dating from the first millennium BCE. These texts were thought to provide examples of good government and social harmony that still were relevant in the 1500s and 1600s. In this view of the world, the emperor ruled over the entire civilized world, with the approval, determined by omens but especially by the acquiescence of elites and common people, of a heaven that was more remote and sky-like than god-like. His key duties were to select officials of the highest learning and morality, to allow them to govern paternally over the common people, and to listen to their advice. The common people would live in their families and villages in harmony of superior and inferior, of old and young.

The places of trade and profit-seeking in such a world view were ambiguous. The same classical text might counsel against profit-seeking, especially by rulers, and praise the benefit to ordinary people of being able to trade goods of which they had too much for others they needed. In Ming times, as the rural economy recovered from the destruction of the Yuan-Ming wars, specialization of production and trade among regions grew. The scholar-officials did not oppose this trend, but their education and values did not give them much guidance in dealing with it.

In the late 1500s China's need for silver in this expanding commercial economy and the demand in other parts of the world for the country's silks, porcelain, and other fine consumer goods were important forces in the flows of the white metal around the world from its prime sources in Japan, the Andes, and Mexico. China's great cities were dazzling centers of commerce and consumer culture. Prices rose, putting a squeeze on officials living on fixed salaries and making them more corruptible. Money talked in late Ming China. Rich people with big estates could keep their land off the tax rolls by bribing officials, often with the help of students doing clerical and go-between work to keep body and soul together until they had another chance to pass the examinations. In the 1590s the Ming state confronted military emergencies in several directions, including Hideyoshi's invasion of Korea, and was in desperate need of increased revenue. Scholar-officials favored limited government and low taxes as matters of principle, and were not of much help in such a situation.

But from the beginnings of the Ming, emperors had escaped from their dependence on scholar-officials by turning to the eunuchs who were supposed to serve only within the palaces. Now, in the 1590s, eunuch commissioners were sent out to the provinces to find and tax the sources of income that so obviously were present in the thriving commercial economy—mines, foreign trade, silk production, and much more. Scholar-officials withdrew from office in protest. Examination candidates demonstrated outside the examination halls. Some scholars, deploring the high spending and unconventional behavior of others, gathered in academies to intensify their Confucian moral practice and to draft petitions against bad government. The result was a spiral of budget deficits, bad government, and increased imperial reliance on the eunuchs, who had none of the scholar-officials' high-principled moral autonomy. It reached a peak in 1621–1627, in the reign of an emperor who preferred carpentry to ruling and left government almost entirely in the hands of a eunuch dictator. Protesting officials were beaten in public in the front courtyard of the palace or tortured to death in the headquarters of the eunuch special police.

One of the cost-cutting measures of the 1620s government was the closing of a large, efficient system of government post stations for the use of officials moving from place to place and the transmission of official correspondence. Especially in poor parts of the country, this threw a large number of porters, horse grooms, and others out of work. Large rebellions broke out, especially in the northwestern province of Shaanxi, promising liberation from corrupt rule and unjust taxation. One of the most important rebel leaders, Li Zicheng, had been dismissed from his

employment in a postal station in a cost-cutting drive. In other areas rebels followed the teachings of White Lotus Buddhism, prophesying the coming of a new millennium of peace and justice.

At the same time, a major external challenge arose on the northeast frontier of the empire, in what is now northeast China. The Jurchen people had ruled north China as the Jin Dynasty from 1127 to 1234. They had made cynical use of their formally subordinate relations with the Ming rulers to send big embassies to Beijing and extort presents and trade privileges. After 1600, one branch of the Jurchen gave themselves a new name, Manchu, a new organization, in which the entire population was enrolled under military units called the Eight Banners, and even a new alphabet for writing their language. In 1616 their ruler proclaimed himself emperor of the Later Jin Dynasty, claiming continuity with the Jin who had ruled north China in the 1100s. In 1618 the Manchus conquered a Ming frontier town. Chinese local officials and frontier soldiers, as well as Mongol leaders, joined them; soon there were Chinese and Mongol units in the Eight Banners.

Under a new emperor after 1628, some Chinese hoped that the Ming would find the competence and resources to face these internal and external threats. But good men who tried to work within the system found themselves constantly undercut by factional infighting and bad policy. Rebels were allowed to "surrender," but simply left in their camps to recuperate and re-supply, and they revolted again in less than a year. A last stand against the advancing Manchu power unraveled in incompetence and defection in 1642. In 1644 the rebel commander Li Zicheng took Beijing, and the last Ming emperor hanged himself on Prospect Hill north of the palace. According to one account, he wrote, "May the bandits dismember my corpse and slaughter my officials, but let them not despoil the imperial tombs nor harm a single one of our people."[2] The Ming general at the pass where the Great Wall meets the ocean called on the Manchus to help him drive out the rebels. They came, the rebels fled after only ten weeks in Beijing, and the Manchu prince regent for the boy emperor proclaimed that the Great Qing Dynasty had come to power and would restore law and order and avenge the death of the Ming emperor.

The collapse of the political order of the Ming had let loose all the conflicts and angers of a commercializing, rapidly changing society. Bondage of farm workers on the land, already in decline, was shattered beyond recovery by revolts of bondservants, especially in the lower Yangzi area. Local rich people were attacked, their storehouses pillaged. Bandits claimed they were robbing the rich to give to the poor. It was not just the elite that was terrified by banditry and disorder; many ordinary people wanted nothing more than peace, quiet, and safety. But it was the elite that was most terrified, had the most to lose, and had the most ideas and experience about how to restore order and how to take advantage of that restoration.

The Chinese elite had very highly developed practices of bureaucratic recruitment and administration, which vastly eased its efforts to restore order and ensured that succeeding generations would have opportunities to rise to office and to modify the system to fit changed conditions. China's ordinary people occasionally saw chances to give a son a good education and see him rise to office, but more often took advantage of peace and prosperity by taking part in the production of the world's finest craft goods and the management of a remarkably sophisticated commercial economy.

But in 1644 to 1645 the questions were whether anyone would be able to mobilize the angers unleashed, and who could benefit from the law-and-order reaction. As almost everywhere in the world of the 1600s, the question took a monarchical form: Who would rule? That was of course not just a matter of superior force, but of wide acceptance. If any would-be ruler had been ready to promise radical redistribution of wealth, he might have gained a large following of the poor, and even of some struggling scholars who had resented the lavish wealth and corruption of the late Ming. After Li Zicheng was driven out of Beijing, no such leader emerged, with the possible exception of the rebel leader Zhang Xianzhong in Sichuan, who does not seem to have discriminated much between rich and poor in his killing sprees. At several places in central and south China, princes of the old Ming imperial house attempted to claim that they were the legitimate successors to the emperor who had died in Beijing and to form "Ming Loyalist" governments. Sometimes these governments were in conflict with each other. Always they were torn apart by the old factions, pro- and anti-eunuch, of late Ming politics. Always they were hostage to the semi-independent military commanders who supported them or betrayed them. None had anything like a chance to provide law and order to the people over whom it claimed to rule.

It was in this situation that the forces of the new Qing Dynasty chased Li Zicheng west from Beijing, his forces fell apart, and he apparently was killed. (That is, in the west, not in Beijing.) They moved their armies south toward the rich fields and cities of the lower Yangzi, adding to their forces defecting units of the Ming armies, local militias, and strongmen of every kind, many of whom were brought under the severe

Ming defenders of a fortress against Manchu attack around 1630 seemed to have a great many firearms. But the Manchus were better disciplined and soon acquired their own muskets and cannon, replacing their customary bows and arrows. Library of Congress, Chinese Division.

discipline of the Chinese part of the Eight Banners system. The Ming generals in command of the wealthy city of Yangzhou refused to surrender, and when the Qing took it, they turned their troops loose in ten days of pillage and massacre.

In 1645 the Qing proclaimed that all men in the empire must symbolize their allegiance by adopting the Manchu hair style, shaving the front of the head and wearing the long hair of the back in a braid, the "queue," a symbol of Qing subjugation that continued to be worn until the Revolution of 1911. In a few lower Yangzi cities scholars and commoners, united by a belief that they should keep intact the body and hair they received from their parents, rose in desperate resistance and were crushed. In other places, however, local people of all classes watched as the Manchu troops rode into town with their outlandish hair and language, saw a few heroic resisters lose their heads, and then watched as the Qing imposed the law and order they had longed for.

By 1650 the Qing forces were in Guangzhou in the far south to stay. A distinctive Ming Loyalist power, based on maritime trade and naval power, emerged along the south coast and hung on to a few bases there until the 1660s, but only once gave the Qing a real scare. Qing forces pushed into the mountains of the southwest, and from 1661 to 1662 pursued the last Ming Loyalist emperor into Burma (modern Myanmar) and brought him back for execution. By then, some officials who had tried unsuccessfully to present proposals for more equitable tax collection and coherent bureaucratic procedures under the late Ming found that the Qing rulers, for all their apparent foreign ways, were more receptive and able to put reforms into practice.

The Qing imperial court at Beijing was still a conspicuously foreign place, where many Manchus spoke little or no Chinese, the imperial family had many marriage connections with the aristocracy of the Mongol people to the north, and Tibetan Buddhism was influential. From 1662 to 1667, Manchu regents for the boy emperor seem to have been hostile to Chinese institutions and to the power of Chinese bureaucrats, but it is not likely that this changed the local government of most parts of the country very much. The maritime Ming Loyalist resistance abandoned its coastal bases but found a new one on Taiwan; the Qing tried to complete the strangling of this challenge by cutting off maritime trade and devastating a wide strip of the south China coast. But these policies were abandoned, and a search for a more sustainable mix of Manchu and Chinese strengths began after the young emperor took power for himself in 1667; he remained on the throne until 1722, the great Kangxi emperor,[3] the key architect of the long Qing peace.

In the 1670s the Qing faced a formidable military challenge from three great Chinese generals who had served them since the beginning of their conquests and had had wide powers in south China; the most dangerous was based in the southwest mountain provinces of Yunnan and Guizhou. As the generals' forces were driven back from 1676 on and the last of them crushed in 1681, the Qing turned to systematic recruitment of the Chinese elite, holding a special examination to recruit scholars for an official history of the Ming and other big literary projects. After the Ming Loyalist regime on Taiwan collapsed in 1683 and the island became part of the Qing Empire, restrictions on maritime trade were lifted.

The Kangxi emperor did not entirely trust the politics of the Chinese scholar-officials, but he learned how to make good use of them. By 1700 the beginnings could be clearly seen of a long boom; frontier settlement in the southwest was very much facilitated by corn and sweet potatoes (new crops from the Americas), copper mines, tea and silk for domestic production and export, and much more. This growth would make China as great a factor in the interconnected world of the 1700s as it had been in the 1500s. The Qing rulers already were turning their attention to their northern frontiers, where their excellent understanding of Inner Asian societies and cultures, their superb cavalry organization, and their new guns would eliminate the threat of the conquest of China from the steppe for the first time in two thousand years. The Chinese examination elite continued to dominate local society and to supply most local officials. In much of China, the only conspicuous signs of change from the late Ming were the shaved heads and queues, but the larger imperial context was quite different, giving China a level of competent government and protection from invasion it had not known for many centuries.

For Europe, the time of troubles ended with the rise of some more unified nations, but the wars went on longer than in China, and some areas recovered only very slowly. The terrors of war in the 1600s were quite different from those of our own time. There were no weapons of mass destruction, no guided bombs delivered from planes safely over the horizon. A musket shot or cannonball could inflict terrible damage at some distance, but most death and injury came hand to hand. The injured had no painkillers, no antibiotics. Amputation of a mangled limb often was preferable to the gangrene that would kill slowly. Maimed ex-soldiers, begging, were everywhere.

For civilians, the passing of an army, even a supposedly friendly one, often meant robbery, rape, torched homes, trampled fields, and slaughtered farm animals. Few armies were well disciplined or firmly committed to a cause, and when pay or bread did not arrive on time, as it often did not, the soldiers would take matters into their own hands. Princes might recruit regiments in their own lands, but they would not want to pay them in peacetime, so they would not be very well trained. The best armies were composed of mercenaries, and for them not only did the soldiers have no hesitation in taking by force the money or bread that was due to them, but the commanders sold their services to the highest bidder.

Much of this was true of seventeenth-century warfare in India or China or the Ottoman realm. But nowhere were the disasters of war worse than in Europe, with its many states and many rulers, and in Europe the classic case of the horrors of war was the Thirty Years War, 1618–1648. This war did not begin the decline of the German lands from their late medieval prosperity and cultural leadership, but it certainly left Germany devastated and politically backward and fragmented until 1800. "Germany" here is a concept out of a later time; in the 1600s there was no single monarchy or unified political structure in the German-speaking lands. Instead there was the Holy Roman Empire, which one later wit remarked was neither holy, nor Roman, nor an empire. The empire consisted of independent monarchies of all sizes, some as large as kingdoms, others just a village or two and the fields around them; of sovereign cities, some of very proud heritage; and of lands ruled by a bishop, abbot, or other prince of the Catholic Church. There were around two thousand such sovereign areas within the empire. Occasionally their rulers or their representatives were summoned to a diet, a plenary meeting that theoretically had to approve all laws and taxes. However, the meetings had proved so chaotic, with constant disputes over voting rights, that the emperors usually ruled without the consent of the diet. But the emperor himself occupied an elected position. There were seven electors of the empire. Three of them were great bishops of the church, who were in turn elected by their cathedral chapters. One of the four non-church territorial princes, the king of Bohemia, was elected by the Bohemian Estates, an assembly of nobles, churchmen, and city representatives. And many of the independent cities were ruled by councils that were elected in some fashion.

All of this dispersal of authority and elective procedure would seem promising beginnings for a political order in which the needs of ordinary people were considered, peace and good order were primary values, and compromise was a basic part of politics. There was much talk in the 1500s and 1600s of the defense of cherished "German Liberties," which meant primarily the ability of each sovereign unit to determine its own fate. After 1618 the liberties proved entirely elusive, compromise never succeeded, and the German people suffered terribly for thirty years. One major source of trouble was that the big powers in Germany were all hereditary princes. This was a common feature of politics in most parts of the early modern world. Often a hereditary monarch took a narrow view of ruling, thinking of little more than keeping intact what he had inherited, or even expanding it, and passing it on to his son or other successor. And anyone who has heard stories of family businesses will understand that when something passes by heredity, sooner or later it will come into the hands of someone whose talents, morals, or interests are not up to the job. Not one major figure among the hereditary rulers of the empire around 1618 was a politician of major abilities. Some of the most competent politicians of the long war were mercenary commanders, whose goals were simply to keep their armies paid and employed and to enrich themselves. Others were foreign rulers and ministers intervening in the German conflict and keeping it going long after most Germans longed for peace.

By far the most powerful hereditary house in the empire was that of Hapsburg. By astute marriages and the good luck of the birth and survival of sons, the Hapsburgs had come to occupy two crucial positions in the European state system, that of king of Spain and that of Holy Roman Emperor—the latter not technically hereditary, but occupied by a Hapsburg since 1273. The revolt of the Netherlands against the Spanish monarchy was the most acute, but far from the only, example of the tension between Hapsburg efforts to centralize ruling power and the proud particularisms of great cities and provincial assemblies. And many of the other conflicts were very much sharpened, as the Dutch one was, by the religious divisions of early modern Europe. By conviction, by strategy, and by influence of the peculiar intensity Spanish Catholicism drew from its background in wars against Muslim powers, the Hapsburgs cast themselves as the great defenders of the Roman Catholic Church. In their responses to the Dutch revolt and throughout the long conflict in Germany, their efforts to stamp out Lutheranism and Calvinism and to support the revival and deepening of Catholic belief were key factors in the polarization of Catholic and Protestant rulers and peoples, the near-impossibility of compromise and tolerance. There also were plenty of bigots and extremists among the Lutherans and the Calvinists, for whom the pope was the antichrist, the agent of the devil at the end of the world. Calvinists and Lutherans sometimes hated each other as much as they despised Catholics. The Calvinist model of control of a community by its elders, not by bishops or rulers, made compromise harder. But the most radical difficulty was that in the Peace of Augsburg, signed in 1555, the Catholic and Lutheran princes of the Holy Roman Empire had agreed to the principle that the ruler of a state could impose his own religious beliefs on all his people. A neighboring ruler with different beliefs could not interfere, but there was no call for toleration of subjects with different convictions.

The history of courts and dynasties around 1600 is full of religious conflict: A Calvinist regent dragging to his services a child prince raised a Lutheran, a prince converting from Lutheranism to Calvinism and trying to exercise his right to enforce his views on his people, and many, many more. In cities and countryside, a Lutheran ruler might find his people swept up in fervent Catholicism by a preacher in the streets, or a Catholic bishop might find the villagers on his estates demanding the right to build a Lutheran church. Only very slowly, in the wake of the horrors of religious war, did anyone of importance in seventeenth-century Europe begin to think that the only solution was for rulers to give up their right to impose their beliefs on their people and to tolerate a more or less wide range of religious belief and practice. The Dutch were among the forerunners in this change, but even in Holland, many were not sure tolerance was a good idea and called for a return to strict Calvinist conformity.

Bohemia, with its capital at Prague, was as full of conflict as any part of Europe. Many Bohemian nobles were Lutheran. But there were many Catholics, and they looked to the nearby support of the Hapsburgs, based in Vienna. The position of king of Bohemia was elective, and the king was one of the seven electoral princes who chose the Holy Roman Emperor. The aging Hapsburg emperor, Matthias, also was king of Bohemia. If on his death a Protestant king could be elected in Bohemia, he could join with the three Protestant electoral princes to make a majority of the seven electors and elect a non-Hapsburg emperor. The Hapsburgs had engineered a meeting of the Bohemian Estates (assemblies) in 1617 at which their Archduke Ferdinand was recognized as the successor to the Bohemian throne. But in 1618 Protestant revolts broke out, and Prague came under the control of a Protestant coalition.

In May 1619 Emperor Matthias died, and the question of who would cast the Bohemian vote in the imperial election became urgent. Most Protestant princes of the empire held back from candidacy, not wanting to antagonize the Hapsburgs or otherwise risk what they already had. But a candidate was found, Frederick, Electoral Prince of the Palatinate, a territory of the Holy Roman Empire with its capital at Heidelberg in western Germany, near the Rhine. Handsome, charming, completely convinced of the righteousness of his own cause, he was not an especially tough or able politician. In August 1619 the Bohemian Estates annulled the election of Ferdinand of Hapsburg and elected Frederick king of Bohemia. The news reached the assembled electoral princes just after they, seeing no alternative, had unanimously elected Ferdinand of Hapsburg Holy Roman Emperor.

The risks that had held back the Protestant princes now became realities. The Protestant cause had been turned into a head-on challenge of Hapsburg power, when many Protestant princes thought compromise still was possible. And for enemies of the Hapsburgs outside Germany, the temptation to intervene in the German conflict, and to keep it going long after most Germans wanted peace, would be irresistible. Finally, Frederick's commitment to Bohemia undermined Protestant control of the Palatinate, a key to keeping Spain from supplying and reinforcing its armies threatening the Netherlands. The result was that the Protestant princes gave Frederick only verbal support. France did no more. He has gone down in history as the "Winter King" of Bohemia, delighting his new subjects with splendid celebrations after his arrival at the end of 1619, out of money by March 1620. Hapsburg forces invaded Bohemia in July; the Bohemian army was crushed and Frederick was forced to flee in November. The Palatinate was occupied by Spanish troops. England and Spain proposed that Frederick abandon the Bohemia venture and return to rule the Palatinate under their protection. If he had accepted, there would have been no Thirty Years War. But, confident in the righteousness of the Protestant cause, he refused and found a few German allies.

As the war continued, there was widespread plunder wherever armies passed. They also transmitted diseases of humans and farm animals as they moved around. Trade was ruined by the insecurity of travel and by minting of low-alloy coins as rulers tried to pay their bills. But a few people became very rich—mint-masters, suppliers to the armies, bankers loaning money to hard-pressed rulers, and above all mercenary commanders. The most powerful of these was Albrecht von Wallenstein. He had broad estates of his own, on which he maintained good order, promoted production, and extracted supplies with ruthless efficiency. His private resources allowed him to keep his troops fed and paid when the ruler for whom he was fighting could not do so; and they allowed him to lend large sums to the Hapsburgs. In 1625, when the Hapsburg Emperor Ferdinand was in great trouble, Wallenstein agreed to raise and pay for himself 50,000 troops. Better disciplined, fed, and supplied, his forces were at least at first less destructive than those of some of the other mercenaries. Ferdinand never trusted him, dismissed him in 1630, and then brought him back on Wallenstein's own terms in 1632. He was murdered in 1634 amid rumors that he was plotting to overthrow the emperor.

But the war now had spun out of the control of Wallenstein, the Hapsburgs, and the German rulers in general. For generations the

Bourbon rulers of France had seen the Hapsburgs as their great enemy, threatening them on their southern frontier, Spain, the northern, in the Netherlands, and parts of western Germany, but had been too distracted by internal unrest to take effective action. Now, under the guidance of Cardinal Richelieu, they began to support all kinds of anti-Hapsburg forces. Despite the militant Catholicism of the Hapsburgs, French efforts against them even had the support of the pope, who was so angry about Spanish meddling in Italy that he declared that the struggle against Hapsburg domination of Germany was not an attack on Catholicism.

Wallenstein's forces gained ground in northern Germany until 1629, when a Baltic coast city appealed for help from Sweden. Most Europeans thought of Sweden as a poor country on the edge of nowhere. But it had gone through major reforms in previous decades, giving it a powerfully united monarchy, and its king was Gustavus Adolphus, a military commander of genius and considerable political vision. Before he died in battle in 1632, he showed signs of wanting to entirely revise the structure of the Holy Roman Empire and of being ready to move toward broader religious toleration. His armies swept down into southern and western Germany. Even after his death, his capable generals maintained Swedish military power in Germany.

Now it seemed that all the German rulers wanted peace, and only the external conflict of Hapsburg and Bourbon was keeping the war dragging on. In parts of Germany, so many peasants had died or fled that the only way an army unit could feed itself was to settle down in the spring, plant a crop, and stay in that place until harvest. Mercenary soldiers wandered from unit to unit, wherever life looked most bearable, not caring which side they were fighting on, not knowing any other life but war. In 1641 the emperor called an imperial assembly and proclaimed he was ready to seek peace. But he still was not ready to give up a policy, proclaimed in 1629, of restoring to the Roman Catholic Church all lands wrongfully taken from it since the Peace of Augsburg in 1555; this goal was abandoned in the final peace settlement.

Formal peace negotiations began in 1644, but the peace treaties were not signed until four years later. There was no armistice during the negotiations, and all sides made delays in the hope that events on the battlefield would favor them, or that some complexity in the negotiations would split their enemies. No one asked the German people what they wanted. In any case, by the best estimates there were 33 percent fewer Germans than there had been when the war began, and in some places the losses were greater. The peace settlement fully recognized the independence of the United Netherlands and the right of each sovereign in the Holy Roman Empire to make his own alliances. So the Holy Roman Empire was effectively reduced to the lands directly controlled by the Hapsburgs, which they were consolidating as a Catholic bloc centered on Vienna. These treaties, and especially the Treaty of Westphalia, are often taken as giving full shape to a European international order of equal and independent nation states, an order that European and American power spread around the globe in the 1800s and that Europe itself now is altering in basic ways. The nation states that had meddled in Germany with such disastrous effect during the war, especially France and Sweden, went on pursuing internal unity and international power, and were joined by England. Hapsburg Austria was a factor in these power struggles, and a formidable new state of Prussia rose out of the debris of the Holy Roman Empire. Until recent times Germans blamed the Thirty Years War for every part of their difficulties with unification and modernity. Both the causal connection and the scope of the devastation have been exaggerated, but certainly the war left Germany broken into many small states with closed ruling circles. And certainly it left the world an unforgettable set of lessons in the horrors of war and the brutal cynicism of foreign intervention in other people's wars.

The peoples of the British Isles watched the Thirty Years War from nearby and occasionally were involved in it. They had their own religious conflicts. But the outcome was quite different. The dramas of seventeenth-century England matter to all of us everywhere in the world not only because they have been very well studied and various theories of change tested on them, but also because one of their outcomes was the emergence of a regime of limited monarchy and real parliamentary power that still is widely influential today, from Ottawa to Madrid to Lagos to Delhi to Tokyo. Assemblies of people with a stake in the prosperity of a city, as in Venice, or of representatives of various cities and provinces, as in the Netherlands, could and did promote an active solidarity that was part of the new shapes of power emerging in Europe. So did the real powers of the English Parliament, but here it was combined with a powerful hereditary monarchy, and questions of relations between the two turned out to be explosive.

This was far from a predictable outcome when Queen Elizabeth died, at the age of seventy, in 1603. Her refusal to marry had been essential to her mystique and her political balancing act, but of course left her without a direct heir. Amazingly, the kingdom did not fall into civil war over a disputed succession; her cousin James VI of Scotland, whose great-grandmother was a daughter of Henry VII of England, was welcomed and generally accepted. A Roman Catholic plot to blow up the king and parliament in 1605 was discovered in time. Its anniversary, Guy Fawkes Day, was celebrated with fireworks for centuries. The drama of the "Gunpowder Plot" moderated for the moment tensions between the prerogatives of the king and the growing parliamentary sense of the rights of free-born Englishmen, and added another layer to the visceral anti-Catholicism that was a feature of English public life for several centuries.

James loved to spend money, and parliamentary consent was needed for most taxes. But the powers of Parliament grew only modestly in his reign, and he managed both to avoid harsh repression of his Roman Catholic subjects and to not antagonize the growing Puritan movement. This balancing act got hazardous in the last years of his reign, after the outbreak of the Thirty Years War. He needed money to strengthen his fleet and army, and to support allies in Europe. But he also needed secrecy and ambiguity in his diplomacy with France and Spain, while growing numbers of his subjects clamored for full support of Frederick of Bohemia, whose wife was James's daughter. Parliament granted funds, but also became a forum for a wide range of protests and grievances by individual subjects; petitions and transcripts of debate, which were not supposed to be open to any common reader, increasingly found their way into print and wide distribution. The king and the bishops of the Church of England insisted that Parliament had no right to discuss matters of religion, but that did not stop the growing bloc of Puritan members from doing so. In 1621 Parliament passed a "Great Protestation," claiming the right to debate all matters of royal policy, and the king rejected it.

James I died in 1625; his son Charles I needed money for war with France and found Parliament resistant. In 1628 he obtained some much-needed funds at the very high cost of his approving Parliament's Petition of Right, which prohibited, among other monarchical abuses, all forms of taxation without Parliament's consent and imprisonment without a specific charge. At the next session, in March 1629, Parliament went over the brink into a full-scale confrontation with the king, refusing his command to adjourn and passing Puritan resolutions declaring all those who advised collection of non-parliamentary taxes or anti-Puritan innovations in the church to be enemies of the kingdom.

Charles dissolved Parliament, arrested several of its leaders, and in a period of prosperity and relative peace managed to rule without a Parliament until 1640. His anti-Puritan policies continued, and the polarization of crown and Parliament spiraled out of control. In 1640 major disorders in Scotland and Ireland made parliamentary funding unavoidable. A Short Parliament refused to grant funds and was dissolved. It was followed by a truly revolutionary Long Parliament, which stayed in power from 1640 to 1660. It granted the king some funds but forced his assent to the trial and execution of two of his chief advisers and to acts that required the summoning of a parliament every three years and forbade the dissolution of a parliament without its own consent. Parliament had gone from being a council serving at the pleasure of the monarch to being an independent source of legitimate political action. This did not mean that Parliament was united as to what to do next. At the end of 1641 a Great Remonstrance summarizing all the accumulated grievances of Puritans and others barely passed; many members were not really ready to take on the monarchy in this way. The king failed to arrest the anti-royalist leaders, and the next proposal from Parliament in June 1642 went further, requiring parliamentary approval of all royal appointments, royal marriages, and changes in religious policy. King Charles rejected it, and Parliament moved to raise its own army. The Civil War that followed was in no way as long and full of horrors as the Thirty Years War on the continent, but there was considerable destruction, and families and communities were cruelly divided. By the end of 1645, the parliamentary forces had won several major battles and were securely dominant. But it was the army raised by Parliament, not Parliament, that was in control; the army purged the Parliament of its moderate members, and the army appointed a court that sentenced the king to death; he was executed in January 1649.

The dominant figure in England in the 1650s was Oliver Cromwell, a Puritan country gentleman who was a gifted military commander and a canny politician, no deep thinker but firm in his rejection of calls for prohibition of any variation in Christian teaching: "Are you troubled that Christ is preached? ... Your pretended fear lest error should step in is like the man who would keep all the wine out of the country lest men should be drunk."[4] In 1653 he became Lord Protector of the Commonwealth of England, Scotland, and Ireland. A Parliament was summoned, but Cromwell found it uncooperative and dismissed it. Gropings for a stable new form of government ended only in 1660, when an army marched out of Scotland, took London, and invited back from exile Charles II, son of the executed Charles I. The survivors of the Long Parliament were reassembled and many of their acts confirmed. In this Restoration period, the tensions between royal powers and parliamentary rights continued, but both sides understood that they had to work within the system, presenting candidates in elections and working within Parliament, forming alliances more and more like modern political parties.

So the polarization of English politics in the mid-1600s had been shaped by the emergence of a new kind of legitimate political power, a Parliament, and that creation shaped a new order after the Civil War.

From the 1620s on, Englishmen had argued about religion and politics in an avalanche of newsletters, printed sermons, and printed petitions. Even parliamentary proceedings had gotten into print. Print aided in the spread of some radical religious visions, in which all people would be equal and Jesus would be coming soon. The Cromwell regime and the Restoration monarchy tried to impose censorship, but printing was fairly low-tech and portable, and was largely out of their control. The Puritans who controlled the Cromwell regime also tried to force people's behavior into narrow channels, forbidding theatricals and dancing at rural festivals; the Puritans may have been right in thinking the springtime dancing around a maypole had something pre-Christian about it, but their prohibition of this beloved tradition won them no friends. This effort did much to undercut popular acceptance of the commonwealth and to make the return of a relaxed, even decadent, monarchy welcome to many.

Russia's terrible "time of troubles" in the early 1600s, and a longer period of confusion and vicious politics from 1584 to 1689, played out on a much larger, less urban, and less well-defined stage, where many people seem to have decided that there was no secure defense against anarchy except a strong monarchy. Before and after those years were two great reigns, that of Ivan the Terrible (1533–1584) and of Peter the Great (1689–1725), each with a brutal autocratic side.

Earlier centuries of Russian history contributed to an autocratic style of ruling. The Russians were converted to the Greek Orthodox branch of Christianity and were deeply impressed by the magnificence of court ceremony and the powers of the emperors at Constantinople. Beginning in the reign of Ivan the Terrible, they used the title *tsar*, (emperor) ultimately derived from the Latin "Caesar." After the Ottoman conquest of Constantinople in 1453, the idea took hold that true orthodox Christianity survived only in Russia, that Moscow was the "third Rome." The tsars passed many of their days in splendid church ceremonies. Fear of pollution of Orthodoxy by Roman Catholicism, which was especially strong in Poland, contributed to a tendency to limit contact with the rest of Europe.

Moscow and the other old Russian cities had grown up along river trade routes that connected the Baltic with the Caspian and Black seas.

The environment was harsh, with deep forests and long winters. To the east and south, the forests opened out onto the great grasslands. The princes of Moscow had begun their rise to power as subordinates of the great Mongol Empire. The Russians were determined to push out onto the steppes and never to face such a threat again. In 1552 they conquered the Khanate of Kazan, a "Tatar" Muslim state of partly Mongol heritage. The ongoing Tatar wars made the maintenance of an adequate supply of military manpower a major imperative of the Russian state. *Boyars*, noble warriors, were granted "service fiefs," not altogether different from the Ottoman timars, in which they had the right to the services and agricultural production of a certain number of peasants, on the condition that they turned out for military campaigns at the head of a force of a certain size. The trouble was that the Russian forests and grasslands were far from fully cultivated, and peasants could and did simply flee from the exactions on boyar estates into vacant land. On the grasslands they developed a distinctive equestrian, semi-nomadic way of life of independent "Cossack" bands of mounted warriors under their own leaders that owed a good deal to their nomad neighbors. The forests provided excellent cover for settlements of religious dissidents. Some forest-dwellers learned how to make a good living trapping ermine and other fur-bearing animals; these people became a significant part of the Russian economy, were impossible to control, and by 1650 had followed the interlocking rivers of Siberia all the way to the Pacific.

A service fief was worth something only with peasants attached; Russia thus was one of many cases in the early modern world—west Africa, Siam, and the Incas among others—where control of people was the greatest source of wealth and power. The tsars supported the boyars with laws forbidding peasants to leave an estate; just as some of the last vestiges of serfdom were disappearing in Western Europe, the Russian peasants became serfs, bound to the land. The process was completed by enactment of a new legal code in 1649. Neither peasants nor landholders had much incentive to increase production on the estates. These measures supported the immense power of the boyars, but did not make them any more submissive to the tsars.

Ivan the Terrible sought to counter boyar power by summoning a national assembly, with representatives of cities, merchants, and lesser nobles, but it was an autocratic improvisation, with none of the power of tradition and precedent of the English Parliament or other western European assemblies. In 1564 the boyars forced Ivan to flee from Moscow, but he rallied his allies and returned. He killed many of

*Tsar Ivan IV "the Terrible" receives a Danish ambassador to his court. The
visitors are brought in through a narrow door to see the tsar in solitary splendor,
surrounded by silent rows of his nobles. Library of Congress.*

his boyar enemies and laid waste the ancient city of Novgorod, which
he suspected of friendliness toward Poland. He withdrew about half
the Russian state from boyar and service fief management, building
up a separate autocratic realm with its own army, administration, and
much-feared police. This provided a stability that did not outlive Ivan;
under his weak son, the boyars were back in control. When the son died

without an heir, the boyars elected a successor, who soon turned to violence against those who opposed him. The worst of the "time of troubles" followed the death of this tsar in 1604, as many boyars accepted the highly dubious claims of a "false Dmitri," said to be another son of Ivan the Terrible. He was killed, but new pretenders appeared, and Cossacks and peasants rose in revolt. Only when Russia was threatened by both Swedish and Polish invaders did the boyars and others agree on the need for unity, convening a national assembly in 1613 and electing Michael Romanov, whose descendants ruled until the 1917 Revolution. This would seem to mark the end of the worst of the time of troubles, but Michael and his successors were not strong rulers. There was widespread rebellion against serfdom, taxation, and corruption in 1648. Reforms in church ritual led "Old Believers," who refused to obey the reforms, to flee into the forests and set up communities that the tsars tried to suppress. In 1670 and 1671 a revolt of Cossacks was barely defeated.

The politics of the court of the tsars at Moscow was dominated by boyar families related to the imperial house by marriage and by the Streltsy, full-time professional soldiers much like the Janissaries of Istanbul. When Tsar Theodore died without an heir in 1682, the Streltsy interfered to demand that two teenage boys, Ivan and Peter, be named co-tsars. But the real power in the court was Ivan's sister, and the much more promising Peter had to stay away from court until 1689, when nobles and foreign officers staged a coup against the sister and brought Peter to full power. He already was showing wide interests in the outside world and a desire to get his great realm in touch with it. As Peter the Great, reigning until 1725, he forced major changes from the top down that opened Russia to the latest ideas and technologies of Europe and made it a major participant in European power struggles.

CHAPTER 7

Toward an Early Modern World, 1670–1700

In 1528 Cabeza de Vaca, a product of a rapidly transforming Spanish-American world, was watching the hunter-gatherers of the Texas coast, who were following one of the oldest human ways of life. By 1700 those peoples, the Karankawa and others, were almost invisible in the historical record; the diseases brought by the Spaniards had taken a dreadful toll, and some remnants were disappearing into the northern frontier of the Spanish-surname, creole society. By 1700 there were not many peoples left in the world whose lives had not been drastically changed by the web of interaction and exchange; the few who remained included the peoples of Australia and New Guinea, the Maori of New Zealand, and the peoples of Hawaii and other Pacific islands. By 1700 Manchu cavalrymen were winning great victories far out in Mongolia, Russian frontiersmen had fur-trading posts all the way to the Pacific, and European fur traders and their Native American allies were following the rivers across the plains of North America.

These new connections opened up a bigger world in people's minds; Jesuits made a fine map of the world for the Kangxi emperor, and a rich man in Amsterdam named Nicolas Witsen collected sources on the Russian advances in Asia and compiled a detailed map of Siberia. A widening world of European power may have made some Muslims more determined in defense of their faith, as when Aurangzeb broke with the tolerant practices of his Mughal ancestors, but it made others, especially in Istanbul, uneasily aware that they had to respond somehow to the new European skills and powers. And those new skills and powers were not only on maps but in people's minds, not just great minds like Isaac Newton's, but those of the people who read travel books, simple explanations of new scientific ideas, and arguments for religious toleration after centuries of religious war. Chinese writers about practical problems of government and Japanese writers of guidebooks to their country's rapidly growing cities also were changing people's values and understandings of the world. Our modern interconnected world had indeed begun to take shape by 1700, with "early modern" trends apparent not just in Europe but in many other parts of the world as well.

Two of the biggest patches of color on a twenty-first-century globe are Russia and China. Both expanded a long way toward their present boundaries between 1600 and 1700. The advance of Russia, which today stretches across eleven time zones, was especially dramatic. The immense expanse of cold forest and tundra we call Siberia takes its name from Sibir, the capital of one of the successor states of the Mongol Golden Horde, near modern Tobolsk, east of the Ural Mountains. The Russian conquest of the Tatar Khanate of Kazan in 1552 opened the way for an expansion beyond the Urals that was very rapid, not at all planned by the rulers in Moscow, and only very loosely under their control. The primary agents of conquest were Cossacks; there also were religious dissidents fleeing repression, monks seeking isolation from a sinful world, peasants fleeing serfdom and not wanting to have anything to do with the Russian state, and even some political prisoners sent to the frontier by the tsarist state, as so many were sent to Siberia in the nineteenth and twentieth centuries.

Cossacks led by Yermak conquered Sibir in 1581 and completed their domination of the surrounding area by 1598. They now set out year after year, following the branches of the great rivers that flow down to the Arctic Ocean, setting up forts at key river junctions and portage points from one river system to another, somewhat like the fur traders of inland North America but in a continent several times larger and with an even harsher climate than modern Minnesota or Manitoba. The native people raised some crops in the short summers, herded reindeer, and hunted and trapped in the great forests. They trapped some of the finest furs in the world, including sable and ermine, and had long been accustomed to trading furs for food, metal goods, and much more, or presenting a tribute of furs to outsider overlords like the Khans of Sibir or the various rulers of the Mongolian steppe to the south.

Russian Christianity faced rival sets of religious connections among the peoples of Siberia. Some of the Siberian peoples were Muslim. The Buryats had turned to Tibetan Buddhism, which was becoming very influential among the Mongols. The Russian state profited greatly from control of the fur trade out of Siberia to the markets of Europe and late in the 1600s was opening a new fur trade to China. The tsars kept some of the Cossacks on the payroll and sent officials to command the garrisons of the little forts.

In the 1640s settlers at a frozen outpost called Yakutsk on the Lena River, where no grain could be grown, heard of grain-growing areas along the Amur River to the south. They thought it would be wonderful if they could open a trade there and buy grain. A first expedition in 1643 was a disaster, ending with Cossacks plundering local towns for food and reports that they had eaten both captives and fellow Cossacks. Further expeditions were almost as brutal, but they did lead to a Russian settlement at Albazin on the Amur.

These few hundred frontiersmen, a third of the way around the earth by land from Moscow, acted as if they were dealing with yet another small population of hunters and reindeer herders. In fact, they had stumbled into the northern fringes of the homeland of the Manchu people, who in the 1650s were in the late stages of their astonishing conquest of all of China. This homeland, now the northeastern provinces of the People's Republic of China, was a land of varied resources—plains where crops could be planted and herds grazed, mountains and forests full of fur animals and other game and the world's prime source for the medicinal herb ginseng, and rivers teeming with fish. The various rulers of the area long had profited from these riches and traded with Korea and with China. Two peoples from this area, the Khitan and the Jurchen, had ruled part or all of the north China plain from 1000 to 1230 and had provided some very able ministers to the great Mongol Empire.

The Manchus, a formidable reorganization of large parts of the Jurchen people, had much of this territory very firmly under control, knew how to deal with related peoples on their frontiers, and were not about to tolerate encroachment on this frontier of a few hundred wild men out of the frozen north. Building boats for a campaign on the rivers and evacuating local populations so that the Cossacks would not find anyone to rob, they pushed the Russians out of the Amur in 1658. But outlaw Cossacks began to sneak in again about 1665, and in the 1670s the Manchus were fighting for their lives against rebels in China. From 1681 on, with their survival in China assured, they turned again to their northeast frontier, planning carefully, building grain reserves for their own forces, evacuating some local people, and demanding that the Russians withdraw. Moscow tried to send reinforcements, but could not really control its own wild men at that distance. In 1685, three thousand Manchu soldiers besieged Albazin, and the Russians had to surrender again. Again some Russians sneaked back, and there was another siege in 1686, but now both Moscow and Beijing were determined to control the situation and make a peaceful settlement; their envoys met at Nerchinsk in 1689 and signed a treaty delineating the border, requiring the destruction of Albazin, and making arrangements for peaceful trade.

The Qing rulers, led by the brilliant young Kangxi emperor, had shown far more ability to organize and plan than their Russian antagonists. This was partly because the Russians were so far from their capital and so much of their presence was the result of lawless frontier encroachment. But the Qing also had behind them both the formidable bureaucratic and documentary traditions of China and the Inner Asian talent for making a new state and people that the Manchus had shown in the early 1600s. The threat to the Manchu homeland could not be ignored. And both they and the Russians understood that if they did not keep peace with each other, the Manchus might face the Russians allied with the cavalry power of the Mongol peoples, or vice versa.

Some Mongols already had been drawn into the Qing structure, which now included Mongol cavalry units and officials. The very powerful and astute grandmother of the Kangxi emperor, the Dowager Empress Xiaozhuang, was a Mongol of the imperial house of Chinggis. And in the 1680s Qing relations with the Mongols had become very dangerous indeed. Galdan, ruler of the western Mongol group called the Oirad, was a brilliant military leader who had been highly educated in Tibetan Buddhism under the Fifth Dalai Lama. He attacked the Mongol allies of the Qing in the 1680s, and by 1690 was in eastern Mongolia threatening Beijing itself. A 1690 Qing campaign into the steppe was badly mismanaged. But in 1697 the emperor himself led a stronger force, and his armies hunted down and killed Galdan.

The Oirads would continue to oppose the Qing under other leaders, but the long-term result of Qing engagement in the north and northwest was the extension of their control out to and even beyond the present northwest frontiers of the People's Republic of China. The Qing controlled and developed this huge area, the modern region of Xinjiang, in part by sending political prisoners to farm there and by using literate prisoners as local administrators, somewhat as the Russians did in Siberia. The local society, unlike Siberia, was educated, urban, and had multicultural links, especially to the world of Islam.

A full map of changes in the world of the late 1600s would show these changes in the continental interior of Asia, but not much in the way of new discoveries by sea, by the Europeans or anyone else. Dutch and English voyagers had seen bits of the coast of Australia but had not seen any reason to stay or come back. The Spanish Manila galleons continued their annual voyages back and forth across the Pacific, but as far as we know, they never discovered the Hawaiian Islands and had only vague knowledge of the Pacific coast north of the tip of Baja California. The growing knowledge of the interiors of the great continents as news from Cossacks, coureurs de bois, and bandeirantes spread out filtered out slowly to report-writers and cartographers.

If we wanted to map changes in the flows of goods and peoples across oceans in the late 1600s, we would have to notice the growing streams of voluntary Chinese settlers in Southeast Asia and of involuntary African migrants to the new world. Brazilian sugar and tobacco, West Indian sugar, North American grain and timber, and Indian cotton and silk fabrics were among the growing streams of goods moving long distances by sea. Europe was just beginning to develop a taste for tea from China and coffee from Yemen. The great Inner Asian trade routes that we call the Silk Road were not growing, and they were increasingly threatened by disorder as the Russians advanced into Central Asia and the roads of the Mughal, Safavid, and Ottoman empires became less safe for merchant caravans.

In the world of the late 1600s, the newest and probably the safest great city was Edo (now Tokyo). By no means new, but still very impressive in its splendid buildings, rich markets, and variety of peoples and religions, was Istanbul. Newer and sharing Islamic concepts of rule and secure roles for non-Muslim peoples were Delhi, the Mughal capital, and Isfahan, in Iran. Amsterdam had gained wealth and power by functioning as an entrepot, a city where goods from around the world were readily available. By 1700 Amsterdam still was a prosperous center of trade and finance, but the fastest growing entrepot was London. All these cities functioned to some degree as entrepots: Istanbul most because of its location at a crossroads and Edo only for trade within Japan because of the severe limits on foreign contact. Beijing was the capital of one of the most sophisticated, successful states of the time and an important entrepot for trade from the northern borders, the prosperous south of China, and the southern cities like Suzhou, still today a great tourist destination near Shanghai, where rich men built splendid walled gardens and shared poems about rural tranquility with their friends while just outside their gates the noisy and turbulent life of a great commercial city, with major silk fabric workshops and occasional labor troubles, roared on.

But cities were not nearly as dominant in this "early modern" world as they are in our times. In the world of the late 1600s, most people farmed and never traveled more than 10 miles from their homes. Technologies of production were sophisticated and adjusted to new market demands but had almost no connection with the changes just getting under way in man's understanding of nature.

Copernicus, Galileo, Newton: These are the most renowned of the scientists who, between 1500 and 1700, laid the foundations for the central roles of science and technology based on science in our modern world. The phrase Copernican Revolution refers to the change from a traditional picture of Sun, Moon, planets, and stars in perfect orbits around Earth to one of Earth and other planets orbiting the Sun and the Moon orbiting Earth, a picture that guardians of Christian tradition found fundamentally at odds with their picture of eternal heaven above Earth and hell below. Thus the phrase Copernican Revolution often is used metaphorically for other and later "revolutions" that seem to challenge tradition. The Copernican Revolution—and the broader "Scientific Revolution" of which it was part—took place in Europe, but became in later centuries a worldwide phenomenon and even before 1700 was the product of global interactions. The world of Islam had preserved classical Greek knowledge of nature and the heavens and had added a great deal of comment and astronomical observation, all of which was transmitted to Christian Europe.

In the wider world opened up by voyages across the Atlantic and into the Indian Ocean, Europeans found everywhere people who knew their own environments very thoroughly, even primitive ones like the Karankawa of Texas, and many who wrote down astronomical observations, lists of medicinal plants, and much more, as carefully as Europeans did. Aztec herbal books were carefully studied by scholars in Rome around 1600. In many parts of the world, Europeans found ingenuity in producing fine goods and saving labor that at least matched their own—elaborate procedures for mining and refining metals and pumping water in China, production of textiles far finer than Europe's in both India and China. But there was almost no interaction between scientists like Copernicus and Newton pursuing deep truths about nature and the world of practical ingenuity and production anywhere, including Europe, until well after 1700. The application of astronomical knowledge to navigation across oceans was a rare exception.

The Polish astronomer Nicolas Copernicus presented his challenge to the traditional view of the cosmos as a limited attempt to purify and perfect the traditional view, and it aroused only a limited response. But a steady accumulation of observations that did not fit the traditional picture had begun; it was carried much further by the Danish astronomer Tycho Brahe, whose king had built for him the best observatory in Europe, and by the German theorist Johannes Kepler, who inherited Brahe's stacks of exact data. Accumulating observation interacted with ever more careful and exact mathematical calculation of orbits, which simply could not be fit into the traditional scheme.

Galileo Galilei was a member of a circle of scientific investigators in Rome called "The Academy of the Lynx-Eyed," its members hoping they would be as sharp-eyed as the lynx. Members encouraged each other in sharp observation in all its forms. Galileo wrote in Italian—a language more accessible to ordinary people than Latin—a brilliant exposition of the new picture of the cosmos. He seized on the first hints of how to make a telescope, and he made one himself, a breaching of the barrier between pure science and making things. He saw things that could not be fitted into the traditional picture of the perfect and changeless heavens—mountains on the moon, moving spots on the sun, four moons orbiting Jupiter. His report on these as "Medician moons" flattered the Medici rulers of Florence, who appointed him their court astronomer and philosopher and distributed his writings and telescopes through their diplomatic channels. But in 1632 the Roman Catholic Church forced Galileo to renounce the Copernican conclusions of his writings. "But they move," he said as the trial ended, and he was sentenced to lifelong house arrest.

Every great tradition has its ways of resisting change and punishing innovators. The Roman Catholic Church of this period, its determination not to change and its procedures for suppressing dissent strengthened by the long struggle against Protestantism, was unique in the centralized, legalistic rigor of its efforts to defend tradition. (We might wonder if in the long run Islam was more effective in suppressing dissent by leaving more scope to the actions of the individual believer, and giving him or her plenty of opportunity to read the Quran and go on pilgrimage to Mecca.) Already the Academy of the Lynx-Eyed had conceived themselves as defenders of the evidence of the senses against a traditional dogmatism that would not pay attention.

Galileo's writings, translated and reprinted across a Europe of many centers and many languages, had made him famous, and the shock of his condemnation convinced many that science and reason had to stand on their own and not bend to tradition and dogma. Printing, organization of like-minded seekers in an academy, court patronage in the multi-centered European world, scientific instrument-making, a passion for mathematical elegance, and the heavy-handed repression of a church feeling threatened by every new idea all joined in this amazing drama.

The urge to understand Earth, sun, moon, and stars was present in all civilizations. The Chinese were very anxious to keep their calendars accurate and predict eclipses, and responded with great interest to new methods brought by Jesuit missionaries. If we look forward into the eighteenth century, we find interest in the new astronomical findings in Japan and in Hindu India. And Copernicus himself seems to have drawn on the tables and new interpretations of the great observatories of Islam, including that of Ulugh Beg at Samarkand. There even was an observatory quite similar to Tycho Brahe's built at Istanbul about the same time, in the 1570s. But this was at the end of the long reign of Suleyman the Lawgiver and enforcer of Sunni orthodoxy. The observatory soon was torn down as a result of factional infighting in the Ottoman court and the criticisms of Muslim religious leaders that it represented too much attention to non-religious learning and too close an approach to astrology. There was similar opposition to the new learning in Christian Europe, but with so many centers of autonomous power, some new patron always emerged to support the astronomers—in Denmark for Brahe, at Florence for Galileo, in London for Newton, and many others.

Kepler had had a rough sense of the elliptical orbits of the planets but had not managed to work out the math, absolutely essential for the combination of exact observation and mathematical rigor that would make the new vision of the cosmos irrefutable. Isaac Newton did the math; his *Principia* (in Latin; published in English as *Mathematical Principles of Natural Philosophy*) of 1687 is the triumphant culmination of the quest begun by Copernicus. Newton was the product of a world that looked a good deal more like that of the modern scientist than Kepler's or Galileo's had. His professorship at the University of Cambridge, where little science was taught, was useful mainly in giving him the time and security to think through some big problems. In his generation, a number of scientific journals were published regularly, especially one in France and one in England, and in both Paris and London there were circles of men interested in investigating the natural world who met to hear papers on new discoveries and interpretations and to see experiments performed. Newton gave one very important paper on optics at the Royal Society, but was too sensitive to criticism for the give and take of the meetings. His great work got published, despite his many misgivings and hesitations, because a lesser scientist of wonderful energy and generosity, Edmund Halley, did the heavy editing work and got some support from the Royal Society. And once the book was out, the summaries and reviews in the intellectual and scientific journals spread its impact, and other writers found ways to present its densely mathematical findings in ways more people could understand.

This is an "early modern" story, and it is easy to emphasize the "modern" and forget the "early." Newton himself was intensely interested in alchemy and in some esoteric branches of Christianity. Far into

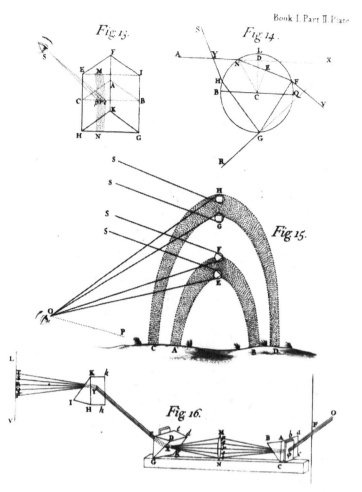

The beautiful diagrams in Newton's works help the reader grasp his mathematical reasoning. This plate from his Opticks (1704) illustrates the diffraction of light through prisms and rainbows. Library of Congress, LC-USZ62-95334.

the 1700s many people rejected Newton's theories. Schools that taught some basics of the new science may have contributed to the technological inventiveness of the 1700s, such as the first steam engines, but the connection between science and technology was much less close than it became in the 1800s. Newton and the mystique of Newton became part of a new culture of hope for science, observation, and criticism of tradition. The institutionalization of science in universities and laboratories also came only in the 1800s. Some historians want to use the phrase "scientific revolution" only for the developments in the 1800s. But still it seems right to say that something basic had happened by 1700, in the "Copernican" change in view of man's place in the cosmos, and in the networks of societies and journals that built the ongoing collective life of inquiry that is the real heart of science.

Isaac Newton watched from the sidelines another revolution, in which we again can see the crucial importance of the multi-centered nature of European politics and of printing and public opinion in these European contexts. Again, the story is one that is important to us because it stands at the beginning of developments, here political democracy, that are crucial parts of the history of all parts of the world in our times. In 1688 the very dangerously polarized politics of seventeenth-century England, which had cost one king his head and many soldiers and civilians their lives in a nasty civil war, came to a very surprising resolution. We call it the Glorious Revolution not because everyone involved acted heroically or selflessly, but because hardly anyone got killed, and the settlement that followed it put firmly in place the rights of an elected Parliament to make basic decisions about government. William and Mary, brought to the throne by the Glorious Revolution, had their positions confirmed by the Declaration of Rights of 1689, which established an elected Parliament as supreme in the fundamentals of taxation and legislation, and set clear limits to royal power.

The restoration of the monarchy under Charles II in 1660 continued the consolidation of a centralized state that had begun under Cromwell. Cromwell was an intelligent and competent politician who hoped to implement broad religious toleration at the head of a military dictatorship with a narrow political base and limited claims to legitimacy. After his death in 1658, it was only a matter of time until the right combination of military and parliamentary maneuvers led to Charles II to return to his father's throne amid widespread rejoicing. The Restoration period under Charles II was an extravagant reversal of Puritan moral repression, as the king led the way in the acquisition of mistresses and lavish living. It was obvious that his court was oriented toward the France of Louis XIV and was sympathetic to Roman Catholicism. Dissenters from strict Anglican belief and practice suffered under many legal disabilities.

The battles of the Civil War in the 1640s, the sieges of towns and castles, the families divided or deprived of their fathers, had given way to sullen repression under Cromwell, then the reversal of the Restoration, and the uncertainties of confiscation and restitution of estates and the settling of old political scores. Paradoxically, it was in the

Commonwealth and Restoration years that foundations were steadily laid for the emergence by 1688 of an England of unprecedented prosperity, a far more important player in European international politics than it had been at the beginning of the century, with a broad elite accustomed to participating in shaping national policy. Religious differences and questions of the rights of crown and Parliament continued to arouse passionate commitment in these years. Landowners worked steadily to improve the productivity of their fields. Policies to promote the kingdom's foreign trade at the expense of that of rivals, especially the Dutch, began under Cromwell and were continued under Charles. London became a crucible of early modernity, with coffee houses where political views could be aired and commercial deals made, a raffish and vibrant theatrical and literary life, and a constant succession of political rumors and dramas recorded in gazettes, pamphlets, and broadsheets.

King Charles II was personally inclined to Roman Catholicism, often in the pay of the king of France, and more or less committed to pro-Catholic policies. But he knew that his people were rabidly anti-Catholic. He converted to Catholicism only on his deathbed. His brother, James, Duke of York, was openly Roman Catholic. The concessions Charles I had made trying to stay on his throne were still in force; the monarchy had permanently moved quite a distance toward constitutional and parliamentary limitations.

But not all Charles's canny and cynical maneuvering could paper over England's deep divisions. They came to the surface quite suddenly in 1678, under the immediate stimulus of fantastic revelations of a "Popish Plot" to assassinate the king, massacre Protestants, and install James as king with a council of Jesuits. When a bill was introduced to exclude James from the succession, King Charles stopped giving way to the extremists in Parliament and dissolved it. The exclusion proposal was truly revolutionary, an interference of Parliament in the affairs of the hereditary monarchy. The "Exclusionists" organized effectively and elected a majority in the House of Commons; they began to be called Whigs, those supporting the monarchy Tories. The polarization that would produce the Revolution of 1688 had crystallized. Charles II now dismissed Parliament and governed without one until his death in February 1685. In 1682 he began to use his wide powers to remodel municipal corporations, removing political opponents and ensuring that they would elect pro-court members of Parliament in the future.

The Whigs were in deep disarray. Their most basic problem was that only a few radicals among them were anti-monarchical, and if they opposed the succession of James, whom did they favor? James, Duke of

Monmouth, the king's bastard son, was popular but not an experienced or reliable leader. In 1683 some radical Whigs were implicated in a plot to assassinate the king and the duke of York at Rye House; some were executed, and the court grew ever stronger.

James, Duke of York, came to the throne in 1685 in a strong position, which his anti-Catholic subjects found worrisome before he did anything at all. He hoped to get some agreement on relaxation of laws against Roman Catholic religious observances and permission for Catholics to hold office in government and army. He thought it might help to extend his proposals for toleration to others outside the Church of England, even the radical Quakers. William Penn agreed with him, but for many conservative Englishmen, the thought of toleration of radical Christians was as repugnant as toleration of Catholics. James began to build up forces under his command, including Catholic troops from Ireland. Many people worried about the parallels with the strong monarchy of Louis XIV just across the English Channel and its persecution of Protestants. James exercised his power to temporarily suspend the anti-Catholic laws, but when he repeated that suspension early in 1688, seven bishops of the Church of England refused to read it from the pulpit and were imprisoned. Huge crowds knelt to receive the bishops' blessing as they were taken to the prison of the Tower of London.

In many parts of the world, a political order was hostage to the chances of birth, life, and death in a hereditary monarchy. King James had no male heir. But on June 10, 1688, a baby prince was born, improving the chances that James would have a legitimate male heir raised Catholic at his court. James's daughter Mary was the wife of William, stadholder of the United Netherlands. William had made it clear that he was willing to intervene in the English political crisis if he received a written request from nobles and influential men, and by the end of July he had one, along with assurances that many men who would not sign such a document would support him. Securing the support of the cautious, decentralized government of the United Provinces in such a risky venture was not a sure thing, but when the French imposed new restrictions on Dutch trade in their ports, Amsterdam came around. A formidable fleet sailed at the end of October, was forced back by a storm, and then sailed again. Swept along by a "Protestant wind," it sailed down the English Channel and to a safe, unopposed landing on the southwest coast of England. William had published a declaration of the reasons for his intervention, and at least sixty thousand copies were being circulated throughout England. His advancing forces encountered almost no armed opposition, and more and more great men came to give their allegiance to him, including some very close to King James. On December 17 William's regiments were in London, and James was allowed to slip away to exile in France.

The ordinary people of London had responded to the excitement, and to anti-Catholic rumor and propaganda, by rioting and burning a Catholic chapel at an embassy and the offices of the king's printer. Committees of officials, nobles, and London merchants were trying to maintain order through the transition. James's flight left the way clear to the throne for William and Mary. The terms were not clear. Had James vacated the throne? Abdicated? How could a Parliament be summoned without a king to summon it or a great seal on the summons papers? On December 26 William convened an informal council of peers and sympathetic members of Parliament. He clearly set the agenda for the meeting, but also sought their advice. The Restoration of 1660 provided the necessary precedents. There would be a "Convention" elected in much the same fashion as a Parliament in response to William's letters of summons.

The Convention met on January 22, 1689. Radical Whigs, heirs of the Exclusionists of ten years before, were ready to simply declare William king. But many others could not tolerate the idea of a purely elective monarchy and wanted a role for Mary by hereditary right. Thus it was that the crown was offered to both of them. One peer said to another, "I look upon this day's work to be the ruin of the monarchy in England, for we have made the crown elective. But there is an absolute necessity of having a government, and I do not see a prospect of any other than this; we must not leave ourselves to the rabble."[1]

The Convention also passed a Declaration of Rights that was presented to William and Mary at the same time as the offer of the crown. It was a comprehensive reassertion of "ancient rights and liberties," including freely elected, frequent parliaments and many limits on pretended royal prerogatives. It became statutory as the Bill of Rights at the end of 1689. William declared that he was not taking the crown on conditions, but the Declaration was read at the beginning of the coronation ceremony of William and Mary on February 13. It could hardly have been clearer that William and Mary had come to the throne by consent of their elected subjects, and on terms set by those subjects.

William came to power in England as a result of an armed invasion, but with very little bloodshed. The early modern world included many who sought conquest, some as lost as Cabeza de Vaca and his three companions and some who triumphed like Mehmet the Conqueror, who rode through the streets of Constantinople. The Kangxi emperor was an administrator and scholar but also a conqueror. Kangxi, heir to a conquering Manchu generation and conqueror of the Oirad Mongols, did not have to arrange a post-pacification election to secure the rights of the Qing to rule China or the Mongols. I do not think the Jesuits who taught him a good deal about European thought, science, and even politics ever told him about the procedures to elect the doge in Venice or about the almost-elective monarchy that resulted from the Glorious Revolution of 1688. He was formed by an Inner Asian tradition that frequently made use of warrior councils and by a Chinese tradition in which ministerial resistance to imperial tyranny had great prestige, and both ruler and ministers were supposed to make the welfare of the common people their main goal. But he would have found formal elections of representatives and formal votes in representative assemblies baffling and repugnant. He might have been interested in the new forms of printing going on in Europe; he was himself energetically promoting a number of history, dictionary, and encyclopedia projects that kept dozens of eminent scholars busy and came out in big print runs that China scholars still consult.

Kangxi had been taught a bit more about matters relevant to the Scientific Revolution, although not about its core theoretical breakthroughs; the Roman Catholic Church still did not accept the theories of Copernicus and Galileo, and the Jesuits, in their writings in Chinese and as far as we know in their teaching of the emperor, stuck to their superior techniques of observation and prediction and stayed away from the big theories. Kangxi liked the observational side; he sometimes took a Jesuit along on one of his great summer hunts and had him set up instruments to measure his current latitude at the end of a long day on horseback. From the 1670s on he could study a great map of the world made for him by a multi-talented Jesuit, showing the latest European knowledge of the world, even of the Americas, all captioned in Chinese. Beginning in 1700, he employed the Jesuits to compile a great atlas of maps of his empire, where their superior skills in surveying and laying findings out on grids of latitude and longitude would be so useful. Jesuits sometimes led surveying and compilation parties to outlying provinces, and otherwise instructed the Chinese and Manchus who would do the investigations. In traditional Chinese statecraft there was a strong sense that maps were of strategic importance and that foreigners entering the empire had to be carefully restricted in their movements because they might be trying to spy out invasion routes. Kangxi knew all this, but he knew who had the skills he needed.

The Jesuits told Kangxi as little as possible about the religious divisions that had plagued Europe in the 1500s and 1600s. If we are right in thinking that one factor in those troubles was localized resistance and resentment toward a rich and highly centralized Roman Catholic Church, Kangxi was about to have a somewhat relevant experience of his own. Off and on through the 1600s, Church authorities in Rome had tried to sort out missionary controversies on the appropriateness of Jesuit compromises with Chinese traditions of belief and ceremony. The Roman authorities never doubted their right to make such decisions, despite their own profound ignorance of China. In 1705 they sent a papal emissary to Beijing, who outraged the emperor by his ignorance and his insistence on making decisions about what was right for the missionaries and their converts. Kangxi's dismissal of the envoy and his decisions, and the papacy's intransigent reactions, doomed Chinese Catholicism to more than a hundred years of formally illegal survival, largely in remote rural areas.

But still the Jesuits were allowed to continue their astronomical and mapmaking work for the great emperor and his successors. The Kangxi emperor learned much from the Jesuits. He ordered them to write books on western astronomy and Euclid's geometry in the Manchu language, and sometimes spent several hours a day studying with them. With them he studied cannon-forging and also had some lighter moments, with a water fountain that was linked to an organ and a few harpsichord lessons. He learned to measure distances and the angles of riverbanks; when he went on an inspection tour along the Grand Canal, he demonstrated these methods to his officials. In the Chinese tradition water control was one of the most serious responsibilities of the ruler and the officials, in legend ever since the sage Emperor Yu controlled a great flood before 2000 BCE. An emperor who was himself a conqueror, heir to two cultures and two languages, Chinese and Manchu, was reaching out to another culture and to strangers who spoke other languages and had beliefs he did not share, to improve his officials' work on one of their most important traditional duties. The Qing rulers knew how to shape a changing world in their own ways and how to choose among what other peoples had to offer in a moving, changing, interactive early modern world.

Chronology

1453
Ottomans take Constantinople/Istanbul

1492
Christian rulers take Granada, completing conquest of Iberian Peninsula

1492
Columbus crosses the Atlantic, begins to explore the Caribbean

1498
Vasco da Gama reaches India by sea, around Africa

1500–1523
Sri Krishna Caitanya's devotional revival

1502–1524
Reign of Shah Ismail, founder of Safavid dynasty, Iran

1509–1547
Reign of Henry VIII, England; he breaks with Roman Catholic Church, 1533–35

1517
Ottomans take Cairo

1517–1520
Martin Luther breaks with Roman Catholic Church

1521
Hernán Cortés takes Tenochtitlán (modern Mexico City)

1522–1527
Late teachings of Wang Yangming

1530s
Ignatius Loyola founds the Society of Jesus (Jesuits)

1533–1535
Pizarro conquers Inca Empire (modern Peru)

1533–1584
Reign of Ivan IV "the Terrible" in Russia

1556–1605
Reign of Akbar of Mughal dynasty, India

1558–1603
Reign of Elizabeth I, England

1567–1609
The Netherlands revolts against Spanish rule and establish the United Provinces

1592–1598
Hideyoshi invades Korea

1601
Tokugawa Ieyasu victorious at battle of Sekigahara, establishes Shogunate that rules Japan until 1868

1602
Dutch East India Company founded

1607
English settle at Jamestown

1608
French settle at Quebec

1618–1648
Thirty Years War in Europe

1627–1673
Wars between north (Le and Trinh) and south (Nguyen) in Vietnam

1643–1715
Reign of Louis XIV, France

1644
Manchus take Beijing, establish Qing dynasty

1649–1660
Abolition of English monarchy, "protectorate" under Oliver Cromwell

1662–1722
Reign of Kangxi emperor of Qing dynasty, China

1658–1707
Reign of Aurangzeb, Mughal dynasty,
India

1682–1725
Reign of Peter the Great, Russia

1687
Newton publishes *Principia*

1688
"Glorious Revolution" in England over-
throws James II, confirms rights of Parliament

Notes

PROLOGUE

1. Álvar Núñez Cabeza de Vaca, "Account of the Disasters," in Alex D. Krieger, *We Came Naked and Barefoot: The Journey of Cabeza de Vaca Across North America* (Austin: University of Texas Press, 2002), 199–200.

CHAPTER 1

1. Giacomo Tedaldi, untitled, in J. R. Melville Jones, ed. and trans., *The Siege of Constantinople 1453: Seven Contemporary Accounts* (Amsterdam: Adolf M. Hakkert, 1972), 6.
2. "Shii," "Shi'i," and "Shi'a" are other spellings frequently found in Western-language writings.
3. Kathryn Babayan, *Mystics, Monarchs, and Messiahs: Cultural Landscapes of Early Modern Iran* (Cambridge, MA: Harvard University Press, 2002): xxviii, 312.
4. Modern Iran is also called Persia in many books. "Persian" is used here only for the language, modern Farsi.
5. Wheeler M. Thackston, trans. and ed., *Baburnama: Memoirs of Babur, Prince and Emperor* (Washington, DC: Freer Galley of Art and Arthur M. Sackler Gallery, Smithsonian Institution, and New York: Oxford University Press, 1996), 333–50.
6. This is Banda Aceh, still an Islamic stronghold. It was devastated during the tsunami of Dec. 26, 2004.
7. The great French scholar Fernand Braudel showed how much the two sides of the sea had in common.

CHAPTER 2

1. Columbus's journal, quoted in Samuel Eliot Morison, *Christopher Columbus, Mariner* (New York: Mentor, 1956), 114.
2. Bernal Díaz del Castillo, A. P. Maudslay, trans., *The Discovery and Conquest of Mexico, 1517–1521* (New York: Da Capo, 1996), 190–91.
3. Octavio Paz, trans. by Margaret Sayers Peden, *Sor Juana, or the Traps of Faith* (Cambridge, MA: Harvard University Press, 1988), 157.
4. Gomes Eanes de Zurara, quoted in Peter Russell, *Prince Henry "the Navigator": A Life* (New Haven, CT: Yale University Press, 2001), 246.
5. The kingdom of the Congo was near the mouth of the great Congo River, in the far north of modern Angola.
6. Sanjay Subrahmanyam, *The Portuguese Empire in Asia: A Political and Economic History* (London: Longman, 1993), 59.
7. Diary of the da Gama voyage, quoted in Joan-Pau Rubiés, *Travel and Ethnology in the Renaissance: South India Through European Eyes, 1250–1625* (Cambridge and New York: Cambridge University Press, 2000), 166.
8. Gauvin Alexander Bailey, *Art on the Jesuit Missions in Asia and Latin America, 1542–1773* (Toronto: University of Toronto Press, 1999), 123.

CHAPTER 3

1. Wayne Shumaker, *The Occult Sciences in the Renaissance: A Study in Intellectual Patterns* (Berkeley: University of California Press, 1972), 225–32, quote on 225.
2. The widely recognized "Krishna" is used here in place of the more correct "Krsna." "Sri" means roughly "Venerable."
3. Edward C. Dimock Jr., trans. and commentary, *Caitanya Caritmrta of Krsnadasa Kaviraja: A Translation and Commentary* (Cambridge, MA: Harvard University Press, 1999), 134.
4. Wing-tsit Chan, trans., *Instructions for Practical Living and Other Neo-Confucian Writings by Wang Yangming* (New York: Columbia University Press, 1963), 193, 239.
5. Richard Marius, *Martin Luther: The Christian Between God and Death* (Cambridge, MA: Harvard University Press, 1999), 53.
6. Elizabeth Eisenstein, *The Printing Revolution in Early Modern Europe* (Cambridge: Cambridge University Press, 1983), 150.
7. Marius, *Martin Luther*, 294. The words do not appear in the earliest records but certainly convey his meaning.
8. Village of Wendelstein in Franconia, Germany, 1524, quoted in Peter Blickle, "Communal Reformation: Zwingli, Luther, and the South of the Holy Roman Empire," in R. Po-chia Hsia, ed., *The Cambridge History of Christianity: Reform and Expansion, 1500–1660* (Cambridge: Cambridge University Press, 2007), 75–69, 80.

CHAPTER 4

1. Josiah Child, *A Discourse of the Nature, Use, and Advantages of Trade* (London: Randal Taylor, 1694), 30.
2. Alessandro Valignano, S.J. and Richard Cocks, both quoted in Conrad Totman, *Early Modern Japan* (Berkeley: University of California Press, 1993), 9–40.
3. Paul G. Stanwood, "The Prayer Book as Literature," in Charles Hefling and Cynthia Shattuck, eds., *The Oxford Guide to the Book of Common Prayer* (New York: Oxford University Press, 2006), 140–49, at 143.
4. "To the Troops at Tilbury, 1588," in George P. Rice Jr., ed., *The Public Speaking of Queen Elizabeth: Selections from Her Official Addresses* (New York: Columbia University Press, 1951), 96–97.

CHAPTER 5

1. Mary Druke Becker, "Linking Arms: The Structure of Iroquois Intertribal Diplomacy," in Daniel J. Richter and James R. Merrell, ed., *Beyond the Covenant Chain: The Iroquois and their Neighbors in Indian North America, 1600–1800.* (University Park: Pennsylvania State University Press, 2002), 29–39, at 29. The Mohawks and the Algonquins were two of the constituent groups of the Iroquois.
2. Richard L. Haan, "Covenant and Consensus: Iroquois and English, 1676–1760," in Richter and Merrell, 41–57, at 49.
3. Margaret R. Conrad and James K. Hiller, *Atlantic Canada: A Concise History* (Don Mills, Ontario: Oxford University Press, 2006), 31, 33.
4. William Penn, *Letter to the Committee of the Free Society of Traders* (London, 1683), quoted in Wills, *1688: A Global History* (New York: Norton, 2001), 204.

CHAPTER 6

1. Nicolas Trigault, S. J., quoted in Donald F. Lach and Edwin J. Van Kley, *Asia in the Making of Europe*, Volume III in four books (Chicago: University of Chicago Press, 1993), 1582.

2. Frederic Wakeman Jr., "The Shun Interrregnum of 1644," in Jonathan D. Spence and John E. Wills Jr., eds., *From Ming to Ch'ing: Conquest, Region, and Continuity in Seventeenth-Century China* (New Haven, CT: Yale University Press, 1979), 39–87, at 51.

3. Kangxi actually was the designation of the years of his reign, not the man; "the xx emperor" is standard usage for Ming and Qing emperors.

4. Christopher Hill, *God's Englishman: Oliver Cromwell and the English Revolution* (New York: Harper and Row, 1970), 126.

CHAPTER 7

1. Wills, *1688*, 192.

Further Reading

GENERAL WORKS AND PROLOGUE

Cameron, Euan, ed. *Early Modern Europe: An Oxford History*. New York: Oxford University Press, 1999.

Christian, David. *Maps of Time: An Introduction to Big History*. Berkeley: University of California Press, 2004.

Krieger, Alex D. *We Came Naked and Barefoot: The Journey of Cabeza de Vaca across North America*. Austin: University of Texas Press, 2002.

Lieberman, Victor. *Strange Parallels: Southeast Asia in Global Context, c. 800–1830*. Cambridge and New York: Cambridge University Press, 2003.

Marks, Robert B. *The Origins of the Modern World: A Global and Ecological Narrative*. 2nd ed. Lanham, MD: Rowman and Littlefield, 2007.

McNeill, J. R., and W. H. McNeill. *The Human Web: A Bird's Eye View of Human History*. New York: Norton, 2003.

Newcomb, W. W. Jr. *The Indians of Texas from Prehistoric to Modern Times*. Austin: University of Texas Press, 1961.

O'Brien, Patrick K. *Atlas of World History*. New York: Oxford University Press, 1999.

Pomeranz, Kenneth, and Steven Topik. *The World That Trade Created; Society, Culture, and the World Economy, 1400 to the Present*. Armonk, NY: M. E. Sharpe, 1999.

Reséndez, Andrés. *A Land So Strange: The Epic Journey of Cabeza de Vaca: The Extraordinary Tale of a Shipwrecked Spaniard Who Walked Across America in the Sixteenth Century*. New York: Basic Books, 2007.

Richards, John F. *The Unending Frontier: An Environmental History of the Early Modern World*. Berkeley: University of California Press, 2003.

Stearns, Peter N., et al., eds. *Encyclopedia of World History*. New York: Houghton Mifflin, 2001.

Wills, John E. Jr. *1688: A Global History*. New York: Norton, 2001.

CHAPTER 1

Babayan, Kathryn. *Mystics, Monarchs, and Messiahs: Cultural Landscapes of Early Modern Iran*. Cambridge, MA: Harvard University Press, 2002.

The Encyclopaedia of Islam. Leiden: Brill, 2002–. Also available online and in CD-ROM.

Esposito, John L. *Islam: The Straight Path*. Expanded ed. New York: Oxford University Press, 1991.

Matthee, Rudolph P. *The Politics of Trade in Safavid Iran: Silk for Silver, 1600–1730*. New York: Cambridge University Press, 1999.

Nicolle, D., J. Haldon, and S. Turnbull. *The Fall of Constantinople: The Ottoman Conquest of Byzantium*. Oxford: Osprey, 2007.

Richards, John F. *The Mughal Empire*. New York: Cambridge University Press, 1993.

Shaw, Stanford. *History of the Ottoman Empire and Modern Turkey*. Vol. 1, *Empire of the Gazis: The Rise and Decline of the Ottoman Empire, 1280–1808*. New York: Cambridge University Press, 1976.

Thackston, Wheeler M., trans. and ed. *Baburnama: Memoirs of Babur, Prince and Emperor.* Washington, DC: Freer Galley of Art and Arthur M. Sackler Gallery, Smithsonian Institution; and New York: Oxford University Press, 1996.

CHAPTER 2

Bakewell, Peter. *A History of Latin America.* 2nd ed. Malden, MA: Blackwell, 2004.

Bethell, Leslie, ed. *Colonial Latin America.* New York: Cambridge University Press, 1984.

Clendinnen, Inga. *Ambivalent Conquests: Maya and Spaniard in Yucatan, 1517–1570.* New York: Cambridge University Press, 1987.

———. *Aztecs: An Interpretation.* New York: Cambridge University Press, 1991.

Cortés, Hernán. *Letters from Mexico.* Translated and edited by Anthony Pagden. Introduction by J. H. Elliott. New Haven, CT: Yale University Press, 1986.

Diffie, Bailey W., and George D. Winius. *Foundations of the Portuguese Empire, 1415–1580.* Minneapolis: University of Minnesota Press, 1977.

Leon-Portilla, Miguel. *The Broken Spears: The Aztec Account of the Conquest of Mexico.* Expanded and updated ed. Boston: Beacon, 1992.

Padden, R. C. *The Hummingbird and the Hawk: Conquest and Sovereignty in the Valley of Mexico, 1503–1541.* New York: Harper, 1970.

Restall, Matthew. *Seven Myths of the Spanish Conquest.* New York: Oxford University Press, 2003.

Russell, Peter. *Prince Henry "the Navigator": A Life.* New Haven, CT: Yale University Press, 2001.

Subrahmanyam, Sanjay. *The Portuguese Empire in Asia, 1500–1700: A Political and Economic History.* New York: Longman, 1993.

Townsend, Camilla, "Burying the White Gods: New Perspectives on the Conquest of Mexico," *American Historical Review*, 108.3 (June 2003): 659–87.

CHAPTER 3

Bouwsma, William J. *John Calvin: A Sixteenth-Century Portrait.* New York: Oxford University Press, 1988.

Brotton, Jerry. *The Renaissance Bazaar: From the Silk Road to Michelangelo.* New York: Oxford University Press, 2002.

Cole, W. Owen, and Piara Singh Sambhi. *The Sikhs: Their Religious Beliefs and Practices.* New York: Routledge, 1978.

De Bary, Wm. Theodore, and Irene Bloom, eds. *Sources of Chinese Tradition. Volume One: From Earliest Times to 1600.* 2nd ed. New York: Columbia University Press, 1999.

Dimock, Edward C. Jr. *Caitanya Caritamrta of Krsnadasa Kaviraja: A Translation and Commentary.* Edited by Tony K. Stewart. Introduction by Dimock and Stewart. Harvard Oriental Series, Vol. 56. Cambridge, MA: Harvard University Press, 1999.

Goodrich, L. Carrington and Chaoying Fang, eds. *Dictionary of Ming Biography.* 2 vols. New York: Columbia University Press, 1976.

Hsia, R. Po-chia, ed. *The Cambridge History of Christianity, Volume 6: Reform and Expansion, 1500–1660.* New York: Cambridge University Press, 2007.

Levi, Anthony. *Renaissance and Reformation: The Intellectual Genesis.* New Haven, CT: Yale University Press, 2002.

Marius, Richard. *Martin Luther: The Christian Between God and Death.* Cambridge, MA: Harvard University Press, 1999.

Rosenthal, Margaret. *The Honest Courtesan: Veronica Franco, Citizen and Writer in Sixteenth-Century Venice.* Chicago: University of Chicago Press, 1992.

Tracy, James D. *Europe's Reformations, 1450–1650.* 2nd ed. Lanham, MD: Rowman & Littlefield, 2006.

Wills, John E. Jr. *Mountain of Fame: Portraits in Chinese History.* Princeton, NJ: Princeton University Press, 1999.

CHAPTER 4

Berry, Mary Elizabeth. *Hideyoshi.* Cambridge, MA: Harvard University Press, 1989.

Bouwsma, William J. *Venice and the Defense of Republican Liberty: Renaissance Values in the Age of the Counter-Reformation.* Berkeley: University of California Press, 1968.

Brigden, Susan. *New Worlds, Lost Worlds: The Rule of the Tudors, 1485–1603.* New York: Viking, 2000.

Chambers, D. C. *The Imperial Age of Venice, 1380–1580.* New York: Harcourt, Brace, Jovanovich, 1970.

Deursen, T. van. "The Dutch Republic, 1588–1780." In *History of the Low Countries*, edited by J. C. H. Blom and E. Lamberts, translated by James C. Kennedy, 143–218. New York: Berghahn, 1999.

Israel, Jonathan. *The Dutch Republic: Its Rise, Greatness, and Fall.* New York: Oxford University Press, 1995.

Reid, Anthony. *Southeast Asia in the Age of Commerce, 1450–1680.* Vol. 2, *Expansion and Crisis.* New Haven, CT: Yale University Press, 1993.

Totman, Conrad. *Early Modern Japan.* Berkeley: University of California Press, 1993.

Wills, John E. Jr., ed. *Eclipsed Entrepots of the Western Pacific: Taiwan and Central Vietnam, 1500–1800.* Aldershot and Burlington, VT: Ashgate, 2002.

CHAPTER 5

Blussé, Leonard. *Strange Company: Chinese Settlers, Mestizo Women, and the Dutch in VOC Batavia.* Amsterdam: Foris, 1986.

Curtin, Philip D. *Cross-Cultural Trade in World History.* New York: Cambridge University Press, 1984.

———. *The Rise and Fall of the Plantation Complex: Essays in Atlantic History.* 2nd ed. New York: Cambridge University Press, 1998.

Dickinson, John A., and Brian Young. *A Short History of Quebec.* 2nd ed. Montreal: McGill-Queens University Press, 2000.

Pomfret, John E., with Floyd M. Shumway. *Founding the American Colonies, 1583–1660.* New York: Harper, 1970.

Richter, Daniel K. *Facing East from Indian Country: A Native History of Early America.* Cambridge, MA: Harvard University Press, 2001.

Richter, Daniel K. "Ordeals of the Longhouse: The Five Nations in Early American History." In *Beyond the Covenant Chain: The Iroquois and Their Neighbors in Indian North America, 1600–1800*, edited by Daniel Richter and James R. Merrell, 11–27. University Park: Pennsylvania State University Press, 2003.

Rink, Oliver A. *Holland on the Hudson: An Economic and Social History of Dutch New York.* Ithaca: Cornell University Press, and Cooperstown, NY: New York State Historical Association, 1986.

Sheler, Jeffrey L. "Rethinking Jamestown," *Smithsonian* 35.10 (January 2005), 48–55.

Thornton, John. *Africa and Africans in the Making of the Atlantic World, 1400–1680.* 2nd ed. New York: Cambridge University Press, 1998.

Vickers, Daniel, ed. *A Companion to Colonial America.* Malden, MA: Blackwell, 2003.

White, Richard. *The Middle Ground: Indians, Empires, and Republics in the Great Lakes Region, 1650–1815.* New York: Cambridge University Press, 1991.

Wills, John E. Jr., "Relations with Maritime Europeans, 1514–1662." In *The Cambridge History of China,* vol. 8, 333–75. New York: Cambridge University Press, 1998.

CHAPTER 6

Goldstone, Jack A. *Revolution and Rebellion in the Early Modern World.* Berkeley: University of California Press, 1991.

Kishlansky, Mark. *A Monarchy Transformed: Britain 1603–1714.* New York: Penguin, 2007.

Struve, Lynn A. *The Southern Ming, 1644–1662.* New Haven, CT: Yale University Press, 1984.

Struve, Lynn A., ed. *The Qing Formation in World-Historical Time.* Cambridge, MA: Harvard East Asian Monographs, 2004.

Wedgewood, C. V. *The Thirty Years War.* Garden City, NY: Anchor, 1961.

Wills, John E. Jr., and Jonathan D. Spence, eds. *From Ming to Ch'ing: Conquest, Region, and Continuity in Seventeenth-Century China.* New Haven, CT: Yale University Press, 1979.

CHAPTER 7

Jacob, James R. *The Scientific Revolution: Aspirations and Achievements, 1500–1700.* Atlantic Highlands, NJ: Humanities Press, 1998.

Lincoln, W. Bruce. *The Conquest of a Continent: Siberia and the Russians.* New York: Random House, 1994.

Mancall, Mark. *Russia and China: Their Diplomatic Relations to 1728.* Cambridge, MA: Harvard University Press, 1971.

Spence, Jonathan D. *Emperor of China: Self-Portrait of K'ang-hsi.* New York: Knopf, 1974.

Spence, Jonathan, "The K'ang-hsi Reign." In *The Cambridge History of China,* Vol. 9, *Part One: The Ch'ing Empire to 1800,* 120–82. New York: Cambridge University Press, 2002.

Westfall, Richard S. *Never at Rest: A Biography of Isaac Newton.* New York: Cambridge University Press, 1980.

White, Michael. *Isaac Newton: The Last Sorcerer.* Reading, MA: Addison-Wesley, 1997.

Web Sites

African Voices
www.mnh.si.edu/africanvoices
African Voices, part of the Smithsonian National Museum of Natural History's site, offers a timeline of African history from early humans to the present.

Age of Exploration
www.mariner.org/educationalad/ageofex/index.php
Exploration from the ancient world through Captain Cook's South Sea voyages in the eighteenth century. From the Mariners' Museum in Newport News, Va.

Art of the Mughals before 1600 A.D.
www.metmuseum.org/toah/hd/mugh/hd_mugh.htm
Paintings and architecture from the Metropolitan Museum illustrate the skill of Mughal artists.

Ask Asia
www.askasia.org/
Sponsored by the Asia Society, this site designed includes timelines of Asian history during the early modern period and historical maps.

Association for the Study of the Worldwide African Diaspora
www.aswadiaspora.org
The major interdisciplinary scholarly organization on this topic. Links to professional organizations, conferences, journals, and other scholarly resources.

The Atlantic Slave Trade and Slave Life in the Americas
http://hitchcock.itc.virginia.edu/Slavery/index.php
A thousand images of the slave trade and slave life, many of them from pre-colonial Africa.

Center for World History, University of California at Santa Cruz
www2.ucsc.edu/cwh/
Curriculum materials designed for teachers at all levels, and news of conferences and events.

China and Europe, 1500–2000 and Beyond: What is "Modern"?
afe.easia.columbia.edu/chinawh/web/help/about.html
Photo albums, articles, and video commentary by historians Kenneth Pomeranz and R. Bin Wong.

CNN Millennium
www.cnn.com/SPECIALS/1999/millennium
Multimedia website from the CNN Millennium series, with sections on each century from the eleventh through the twentieth. Includes profiles, timelines, maps, and an interesting feature on artifacts. Very global in scope.

Early Modern Resources
www.earlymodernweb.org.uk/
This site, maintained by Sharon Howard of the University of Sheffield, offers links to a variety of sites about the early modern world, which Howard defines as roughly 1500 to 1800.

Forum for European Expansion and Global Integration
www.feegi.org
A scholarly organization strongest on connections around the Atlantic. Bibliographies and teaching materials.

History of Timbuktu
www.timbuktufoundation.org/history.html
Story of Timbuktu and the surrounding area, with many illustrations and original sources. Sponsored by the Timbuktu Educational Foundation.

H-World
www.h-net.org/~world/
The primary interactive forum for students and scholars of world history, very friendly to the concerns of survey teachers and their students.

Maritime Asia, National Museum of Malaysia
www.maritimeasia.ws
Virtual exhibition of pottery found in
seven shipwrecks from the fourteenth to
the nineteenth centuries, with material on
Southeast Asia's maritime history.

The Ottomans
www.theottomans.org/english/index.asp
An informative site on all aspects of the
Ottoman Empire, including art and culture.

Toward a New Age of Partnership, Leiden University
www.tanap.nl
Information, including guides to archives
and studies, on cooperative scholarship
involving Asian scholars and the riches of
the Dutch archives.

World History Association
www.thewha.org
Website of the leading scholarly
organization in the field. Archives of
World History Bulletin and *Journal
of World History*; information for
teachers.

World History Compass
www.worldhistorycompass.com
Links to primary source archives,
highlights from museum exhibits, lectures,
and other events. Covers nearly every
region and period.

World History Connected
worldhistoryconnected.press.uiuc.edu
Newsletter, interpretive articles, interviews
with historians.

World History Matters
www.worldhistorymatters.org
From George Mason University, excellent
information on primary source archives,
guides to interpreting primary sources,
and resources for teachers. The emphasis
is on cultural interaction, globalization,
and the lives of women.

Acknowledgments

A book covering such a broad range of specialized topics incurs a great many obligations to specialists, and never enough. My dedication to my colleagues at the University of Southern California has several levels. In the Department of History, Deborah Harkness gave most helpful comments on the entire draft, and Carole Shammas, Maria Elena Martinez, Edwin Perkins, Azade-Ayse Rorlich, and Ramzi Rouighi commented on chapters. My colleagues in East Asian history in and out of the department, Charlotte Furth, Gordon Berger, Kyung Moon Hwang, Brett Sheehan, Joshua Goldstein, Bettine Birge, and Peter Nosco, all had their early modern moments and pushed me to develop more nuanced understandings of the part of the world from which I inevitably begin my forays into world history. On a personal, non-institutional level, Lucinda Wills and Muhammad al-Muwadda provided, as always, deep insight into Islamic belief and practice. I also wish to thank the anonymous readers for Oxford University Press and everyone at Oxford University Press who contributed expertise to this project, from illustrations to maps and much more, and especially Nancy Toff. I do not name more names because I never knew the names of some important contributors.

U.S.C. is a "public/private" university, basically committed to serving the huge, fascinating, almost ungovernable city that surrounds it, with a strong global sense that especially looks south across the border and out across the Pacific. Global consciousness here is all across the university. Through the Department of History and the East Asian Studies Center, I have worked with and learned from K-12 teachers in the area as they try to negotiate many variations on the "world history turn." Other eminent globalizers from whom I have learned much include Stephen B. Sample, president; Richard Drobnick, formerly vice-provost for International Affairs and founder of a distinguished international MBA program; and Robert Biller, professor emeritus of policy, planning, and development and all-purpose troubleshooter and global connection builder.

Although my dedication is to my U.S.C. colleagues, I must also acknowledge huge debts to the energetic network of China scholars in southern California, to world history pioneers of all kinds in the region—Kenneth Pomeranz, Robert Marks, Ross Dunn, David Christian, and many more—and to the colleagues at branches of the California State University system, especially Northridge and Bakersfield, with whom I have discussed their various transitions to teaching world history, especially to future teachers. What usually emerges from such discussions is that a history department has far more resources for the teaching of world history than it thinks it does, but people need to think of themselves in slightly different ways and talk to each other. Perhaps this book will help a little, if the Luther scholar and the Tokugawa specialist see their preoccupations intersecting in one short book.

Nationally and internationally, the world history community has been exceptionally open to the needs and concerns of teachers at the secondary and junior college levels. Several have served as leaders of the World History Association. They are a constant and stimulating presence on the H-World e-mail users group. There are times when California multiculturalism involves nothing more than saying "Have a nice day" to the Sri Lankan at the gas station or the people at the nice Armenian takeout. But there are times when we have to work on the consequences of religious difference, understandings of family, and echoes of far-away disasters like the Sichuan earthquake. California teachers, kindergarten to PhD, are more on the front lines on these matters than most of us. If some storytelling, comparison-making world history helps them at all in dealing with their globalized classrooms, that will be an extra reward for the scholar facing his or her computer screen and his or her impossible assignment.

Index

religion (*continued*)
  conflicts between, 63
  diaspora from, 99–100, 108
  divine in, 56–57
  in England, 79–80, 134–35, 150–51
  forced conversion of, 18
  in France, 93–94, 95, 99
  in Germany, 128–32
  Hapsburgs and, 129, 130–32
  in India, 20, 44, 54–58
  intermarrying between, 12
  in Japan, 42–43
  in Jerusalem, 117
  in Mediterranean, 24
  of Native Americans, 34, 103
  in Netherlands, 68, 130
  persecution for, 13, 42
  printing and, 16, 65
  reform of, 68
  in Russia, 136, 139, 141
  in slavery, 112
  unity of, 11, 43–44
  women in, 69
Rembrandt, 116
Renaissance
  architecture of, 50–51, 52
  statecraft in, 72
  women in, 53–54
rent, 11
Restoration, 149–50, 152
Ricci, Matteo, 43
Richelieu, Cardinal, 94, 132
righteousness, 65
Rio Grande, 5–6
Riva degli Schiavoni, 24
Roman Catholicism
  in America, 105, 107
  Copernican Revolution and, 146
  corruption in, 64, 69
  Greek Orthodox Church and, 9
  Henry VIII and, 155
  Lutheranism and, 155
Romanov, Michael, 139
Royal Society, 147
Russia
  agriculture in, 141–42
  expansion of, 141
  leadership of, 137–39, 155, 156
  Manchu and, 142, 143
  religion in, 136, 139, 141

Sabbatai Sevi, 117
Safed, 70, 117
Sahara, 36
sailing permits, 40
Saint Lawrence, 105–6
Salimu Sware, 25
Samarkand, 19–20
samurai, 73, 75–76

San Lucar de Barrameda, 1
sannayasin, 56
Sanskrit, 55, 56
São Tomé, 37
science, institutionalization of, 148–49
Scientific Revolution, 145, 148–49
Sekigahara, 155
Seljuk, 10
Senegal, 25
Separatists, 101
Sephardim, 116, 117
serfdom, 137
settlers, American, 97, 100–107, 108, 155
Shah Abbas, 18, 98
Sha Jahan, 22
Shakespeare, William, 50
Sharifs, 14
Shia, 10, 14–15, 14f
Shia Safavid state, 13, 17–18, 98, 155
Shivaji, 22
Siberia, 140, 141
Sikhs, 58–59
silk, 40, 47
Silk Road, 19
silver
  in China, 47, 98, 114, 121
  economic effect of, 119
  in Mexico, 32
  in Potosí, 33, 33f
  trading of, 47–48
slavery
  in Africa, 108–10
  in Americas, 4, 27, 34, 96, 108, 112
  boats for, 111f
  in Brazil, 45, 109, 112
  in Congo, 37
  culture in, 111–12
  in England, 110
  escape from, 112
  life expectancy in, 110
  marriage in, 110, 112, 117–18
  Mediterranean, 24
  of Native Americans, 4
  Portuguese, 36, 37, 109, 110
  religion in, 112
  in Spain, 1
  for sugar cane farming, 45, 46, 109
  for tobacco farming, 101
  web site on, 164
Slaves' Quay, 24
smallpox, 27
Smithsonian National Museum of Natural History, 164
Society of Jesus. *See* Jesuits
Songhay, 24–25
South Africa, 99
Southeast Asia
  agriculture in, 87–88, 89

The
New
Oxford
World
History